PYROTECHNICS
ON THE PAGE

PYROTECHNICS
ON THE PAGE
Playful Craft That Sparks Writing

RALPH FLETCHER

Foreword by Katie Wood Ray

Stenhouse
PUBLISHERS

www.stenhouse.com

Stenhouse Publishers
www.stenhouse.com

Credits:

pages xi, 7: From *Hello, Harvest Moon* by Ralph Fletcher, illustrated by Kate Kiesler. Copyright © 2003. Reprinted with permission of Clarion Books, a division of Houghton Mifflin Harcourt, Inc.

page 4: From *Twilight Comes Twice* by Ralph Fletcher, illustrated by Kate Kiesler. Copyright © 1997. Reprinted with permission of Clarion Books, a division of Houghton Mifflin Harcourt, Inc.

pages 29, 149: "Rosie's Book of Sayings," from *The Muses Among Us: Eloquent Listening and Other Pleasures of the Writer's Craft* by Kim Stafford. Copyright © 2003. Reprinted with permission of The University of Georgia Press.

page 36: "Symmetricats," copyright © 2009 by Betsy Franco, "Illustrations" by Michael Wertz, copyright © 2009 by Michael Wertz, from *A Curious Collection of Cats* by Betsy Franco, illustrations by Michael Wertz. Used by permission of Tricycle Press, an imprint of the Crown Publishing Group, a division of Random House, Inc.

page 66: "No dramatic event, just a mini-series," by Dan Shaughnessy. *The Boston Globe*, August 29, 2007. Copyright © 2007. Reprinted with permission of the author.

pages 74, 141: From *Amos & Boris* by William Steig. Copyright © 1971 by William Steig. Printed by permission of Farrar, Straus and Giroux, LLC.

page 80: "Bad Weather," from *A Writing Kind of Day: Poems for Young Poets* by Ralph Fletcher, illustrated by April Ward. Copyright © 2005. Reprinted with permission of Boyds Mills Press.

page 155: From *Once Upon a Twice* by Denise Doyen, illustrated by Barry Moser, copyright © 2009 by Denise Doyen. Used by permission of Random House Children's Books, a division of Random House, Inc.

page 156: "Flying in the Face of Reason," by Rick Reilly. *Sports Illustrated*, February 19, 2001. Copyright © 2001. Reprinted with permission of Sports Illustrated, Inc.

pages 158–160: "A Balding Pig," "There Was an Old Woman," "Epitaph for a Pitcher," and "Epitaph for Pinocchio" by J. Patrick Lewis, unpublished poems. Used with permission of the author.

pages 158–162: Selected poems from *Countdown to Summer* by J. Patrick Lewis, illustrated by Ethan Long. Little, Brown Books for Young Readers. Copyright © 2009. Reprinted with permission of the author.

pages 158–162: Selected poems from *A Hippopotamusn't: And Other Animal Poems* by J. Patrick Lewis, illustrated by Victoria Chess. Puffin Books. Copyright © 2009. Reprinted with permission of the author.

Library of Congress Cataloging-in-Publication Data

Fletcher, Ralph J.
Pyrotechnics on the page : playful craft that sparks writing / Ralph Fletcher.
p. cm.
Includes bibliographical references.
ISBN 978-1-57110-783-1 (alk. paper)
1. Creative writing (Elementary education) 2. Plays on words. I. Title.
LB1576.F4767 2010
372.62'3--dc22

2009048755

Cover, interior design, and typesetting by Designboy Creative Group

Manufactured in the United States of America

PRINTED ON 30% PCW
RECYCLED PAPER

16 15 14 13 12 11 10   9 8 7 6 5 4 3 2

for Naomi Shihab Nye,
a writer with rare heart
and clear vision

Contents

Craft Lessons

5+

Foreword

Funny thing, but ever since I agreed to write the foreword for *Pyrotechnics on the Page*, I haven't been able to help myself—I've been thinking *backward* instead of forward.

I keep returning to a cold, snowy Saturday in February of 1994. I was living and teaching in New York City at the time, and that morning I wrapped myself in a blanket and curled up to begin reading the new book all my colleagues were talking about. The book was *What a Writer Needs* (Fletcher 1993), and once I started it, I didn't move for hours. I read the whole book that day, and my teaching has never been the same because of it. I've reread it countless times through the years, and I've shared Ralph's wise advice from it so many times; I immediately think of missed belt loops whenever I explain telling details, and grubs eating grits (till their bodies explode) whenever I talk about finding a place that feels right for writing.

Part of why I keep thinking backward is because I feel, quite literally, like I've grown up with Ralph Fletcher as a teacher of writing. I own every book on writing Ralph's ever published and have built much of my knowledge base for teaching from reading them. I can't imagine where my teaching would be if it weren't for books like *Breathing In, Breathing Out* (1996), *Craft Lessons* (2007), *Writing Workshop* (2001), or the wonderful HarperTrophy series crafted with young writers in mind. Interestingly enough, however, Ralph didn't earn my trust as a teacher from writing books *about* writing. I trust Ralph to teach me because he writes books like *Twilight Comes Twice* (1997), *Ordinary Things* (1997), *The One O'Clock Chop* (2007), *Marshfield Dreams* (2005a), and a whole host of other picture books, poetry collections, novels, and memoirs. I trust Ralph to teach me because he writes words like these, from *Hello, Harvest Moon* (2003):

> *The crops have been gathered. The pumpkins have been picked. The silos are filled to bursting with a million ears of corn. Tired farmers are fast asleep. But something is stirring at the edge of the world. Something is rising low in the trees.*

I trust Ralph to teach me because, well, how could I *not* trust him after reading words like these? When it comes to writing, Ralph is a craftsman in the truest sense of the word.

And now, with this new book, Ralph is poised to teach so many of us once again in a whole new way, and we're going to have a grand ol' time learning what he wants to teach us about playing with language.

In *Pyrotechnics on the Page*, Ralph makes a strong case for the idea that good writers must know how to play—with words, ideas, sound, meaning. He says, "Skilled writers do not always follow the shortest route between themselves and their meaning. Rather, they often deliberately play with language along the way." I suppose I could have simply read *Pyrotechnics on the Page* and taken Ralph's word on this (since I trust him so much), but I didn't have to do that. Since reading this lively, engaging book, I am noticing language play in a way I never have before. My senses have been heightened, and I am seeing writers playing everywhere I read.

In a *Time* magazine cover story about the ongoing woes in the great state of California, I find the clever, playful admonition to "ignore the California whinery."

In *Sports Illustrated for Kids*, I notice an article titled "Hoff to the Races," about Olympic swimmer Katie Hoff.

In *USA Today*, a headline reads, "Paucity of NFL Parity Is Cause for Celebration." And another, same day's edition, "MIT's Latest Engineering Feet Belong to Brown" (star running back DeRon Brown, that is).

Ralph is right on this. The world of writing is wide, and it's filled with writers having a good time with meaning in all sorts of texts. While one might think that language play exists strictly in the domain of "creative" (a.k.a. *light*) writing, one would be wrong. It is alive and well in essays, articles, editorials, reviews, memoirs—indeed, in all kinds of writing whose purpose is to connect with readers. Language play powerfully connects readers to writers because in *getting it*, readers are made insiders in the writer's game.

Pyrotechnics on the Page will become an invaluable resource for those who want to nurture a spirit of play in the young writers they teach, a spirit too often missing in writing workshops, its absence separating many children from the literary models they know and love as readers. Ralph first explains how language play lifts writing, and then he shares specific craft lessons for introducing children to the many "tools" of playfulness, tools such as puns, hyperbole, allusions, and a host of others. By gearing lessons to students in grades K–2, 3–4 and 5+, Ralph helps us see how more sophisticated understandings about language play can grow with children as they move through school and grow as writers. Planners of vertical curriculum will find this organization helpful on so many levels.

With *Pyrotechnics on the Page*, Ralph adds a new dimension to the professional conversation about teaching the craft of writing. I believe you will find, as I have found, that your knowledge base about what makes writing *good writing* will be expanded after reading this book. You'll see some aspects of craft in totally new ways, and you'll enjoy each new revelation as language play is explored in depth. And you'll have such a good time doing it.

Almost two decades ago, the late Don Murray wrote the foreword for *What a Writer Needs*. In many ways, Don's words about Ralph then were a harbinger for what Ralph has given us now. At the very end of that foreword Don says this of Ralph:

"He never speaks down; he is, rather, the writer/teacher at work, looking up with surprise and delight as you open the door of his study. He invites you in by saying, 'Come in, I'm having fun'" (1993, viii).

I'm not sure Don could have imagined, so long ago, just how much fun Ralph would still be having there in his study, at play with words. How lucky we are that he has, once again, invited us in to see and to play.

— **Katie Wood Ray**

Preface

Don Murray once told me he had just published an article that received a negative review in one of the journals.

"The reviewer thought it was too Murrayesque," Don deadpanned, his blue eyes ablaze with delight.

Don was a dear friend, though many other people could say what I am saying: he took an interest in my work, and gave me a rare window into the musings and inner workings of a fine writer.

"Someone should write a book about language play," he remarked to me one afternoon. We were having coffee at the Bagelry, not far from his home in Durham, New Hampshire.

"Language play?" I repeated.

He nodded. "Lots of times I'm tinkering with a sentence or fiddling around with a phrase, and that's when I make a breakthrough. I think playing with language is such an important part of writing, but it's a subject that's mostly been overlooked."

Don died in late 2006. A few months later I dreamed that I wrote a book about language play. In the aftermath of that dream I realized that some part of my consciousness must have been thinking about that idea ever since Don first brought it up. It was a book I really wanted to write.

So here it is: a book about various forms of language play used by writers and how they might enrich our students' writing. I'm certain that the book I have written is not exactly the book Don had in mind when he first mentioned the idea to me. I took his fragment of an idea and pulled it in my own direction. But that's okay. In fact, that's a pretty Murrayesque notion in itself.

Acknowledgments

The pages of this book were fed by many intense conversations with individuals who helped me think through and clarify my ideas.

If these acknowledgments were an orchestra, first chair would be occupied by Philippa Stratton, my editor. Philippa and I have done many books together. I believe that some of them have been fairly easy to edit, but she certainly earned her money on this one. With Philippa's guidance, I went through the revision process several times. Couldn't have written this book without her.

Jen Allen and "Aunt" Pat Johnson read an earlier version of this book and gave it the tough love (emphasis on *tough*) it needed. Their response was enormously helpful. Suzanne Whaley and Kathleen Fay both were unusually generous with their time and suggestions, particularly with the craft lessons themselves.

I am grateful to the following writers who graciously gave their time to reflect with me on the role language plays in their writing: Jon Agee, Louise Borden, Eve Bunting, Chris Crutcher, Denise Doyen, Sheree Fitch, Mem Fox, Betsy Franco, Dan Gutman, Avis Harley, Dar Hosta, J. Patrick Lewis, Kate McMullan, Katherine Paterson, Jerry Spinelli, and Jane Yolen.

Several people helped me to think through various issues in this book. I send lavish verbal bouquets to Ann Haas Dyson, Dan Feigelson, Naomi Shihab Nye, Tom Romano, Dan Shaughnessy, Franki Sibberson, Kim Stafford, and Katie Wood Ray.

I am also grateful to all the teachers and educators who reflected on the place of language play in the classroom. I am indebted to Lonna Bagwell, Gresham Brown, Jessica Butterfield, Monica Charlton, Jo-Ann Gejay, Anne Hankins, Lisa Hansen, Julie Leal, Peter Johnston, Anna Lee Lum, Ali Marron, Karen McMichael, Esra Murray, Tina Nakamoto, Erica Pecorale, Rebecca Shoniker, Dave Schultz, Joel Schwartz, John Signatur, Paula Tilker, Deana Tomes, Annie Ward, and Kim Williams.

I have learned a lot about language play from my editors, especially Nina Ignatowicz and Christy Ottaviano.

I am grateful to these individuals:

Cyrene Wells and her husband, Jim Wells (a punster if there ever was one).

Carol Wilcox. Barry Lane.

James Heffernan, my English professor at Dartmouth who continues to stretch my thinking.

Librarian George Pilling, who put me in touch with several authors who have a proclivity for language play.

Setsuko Tsugihara, who has translated several of my children's books into Japanese.

Thanks, JoAnn.

Nobody taught me more about this subject than my sons: Taylor, Adam, Robert, and Joseph. Separately and together, they wove an elaborate quilt of language play. It's a gift I'll cherish until the end of my days.

PLAYING

AROUND

1

Pyrotechnics and Play

Nowadays it seems you often hear about delivery. A local pizza company advertises that if it doesn't deliver a hot pizza to your front door within thirty minutes, you get it for free. FedEx delivers. A prominent mattress company promises free delivery to any customer who purchases one by a certain date. Red Sox pitcher Daniel Bard can deliver a fastball clocked at 100 mph. President Obama delivered the convocation at Notre Dame. A taxi driver helped a woman deliver a ten-pound baby in the back of his cab.

What do writers deliver?

Writing is a form of communication, a word that can be defined as the process of transferring information from one entity to another. (For the time being, let's leave aside the issue of personal writing, which is less about communicating and more about reflecting or ruminating for oneself.) Writers string together written words, forming them into lines or sentences in order to communicate ideas, thoughts, feelings, arguments, events, perceptions, and insights.

Writers deliver meaning. At least this is how writing has typically been taught. We instruct the young writer to write clear, concise sentences so the meaning (ideas, facts, arguments, information) will be clearly understood by the reader. It is a practical, go-and-fetch-it model, one that conjures up the image of a dog at the beach happily plunging into the surf, retrieving a ball, bringing it back to shore, and laying it at his owner's feet.

Since meaning is the headline act, naturally it gets top billing. And while the actual language used in the writing is acknowledged in most assessments ("word choice," "fluency"), it is mostly seen as a means to the end, like the stick used by a blind woman as she makes her way down the sidewalk. This is an intriguing description of writing, and it certainly has some validity, but it leaves out an important part of the story.

Writers play with language.

Skilled writers do not always follow the shortest route between themselves and their meaning. Rather, they often deliberately play with language along the way.

Such play is not subordinate to meaning. In fact this language play—what I'll call *pyrotechnics* in this book—is often what the writing is about.

I am defining *pyrotechnics* as deliberate playfulness with language used by writers to create a particular kind of effect as well as the specific tools used to create that effect. This term includes but is not limited to the following:

puns and double meanings
invented words
allusions
expressions and idioms
metaphors and similes
hyperbole
onomatopoeia
alliteration

In addition, this book will explore various stylistic techniques that operate on the sentence level, including sentences that break the rules, "reversible raincoat" sentences, very short sentences, and sentences that use a 3-2-1 (or 1-2-3) cadence.

Sometimes when reading a piece of writing we encounter pyrotechnics that, like fireworks on the Fourth of July, make us ooh and aah. Natalie Babbitt's novel *Tuck Everlasting* begins with a comparison that is as unlikely as it is pitch-perfect:

The first week of August hangs at the very top of summer, the top of the live-long year, like the highest seat of a Ferris wheel when it pauses in its turning.

But not all fireworks are meant to be dazzling. Sparklers, for one, attempt a much more modest effect. Some pyrotechnics used by writers are quieter and subtler, for example, exchanging one word in a passage for another to make it sound better and flow more smoothly. An early draft of my book *Twilight Comes Twice* (1997b) contained these lines:

*Dawn illuminates
the empty baseball field
polishing the diamond
until it shines.*

I sent this draft to Nina Ignatowicz, my editor. A few days later she phoned to talk about this stanza. Nina has a strong Hungarian accent so I had to listen carefully to catch all her words.

"I like the double meaning of 'polishing the diamond,'" she began. "But I'm not sure about *illuminating*."

"Why?" I asked her.

"*Illuminating* is a word that calls attention to itself," she said. "It's a real mouthful, five syllables. And it seems rather formal, don't you think?"

"Maybe it is," I admitted.

"*Illuminating* is a seventy-five-cent word," Nina continued. "I'm thinking we might need something a little less . . . pricey. I suggest you take it down a notch."

We talked for another half hour. It seemed slightly absurd to spend so much time talking about a single word. But with a brief text like a poem or a picture book, every word matters. I knew that the sound/feel/flow of the language would be every bit as important as the book's subject. I assured Nina that I would rethink my choice of *illuminating*, and hung up.

Experience had taught me to trust Nina's ear, so I read and reread the stanza, both separately and in context with the other stanzas. Gradually I began to realize that she was right—*illuminating* was not the right word. I began to play around with other possibilities, auditioning simpler words as possible replacements. Here's the final version:

Dawn slowly brightens
the empty baseball field,
polishing the diamond
until it shines.

We write with the ear as much as with the eye or the mind. I believe that writing teachers and student writers might do well to shift attention from the *what* (subject/meaning) to the *how* (language). While constructing a text, skilled writers continually ask themselves:

Does this sentence have the sound and rhythm I want?
Do I want the words in this sentence to have a smooth flow? Or (if the content is disturbing, for instance) do I want it to sound discordant and jarring?

What effect is created by having a long sentence followed by a smaller one?

What puns or double meanings could be teased out by altering this common phrase or familiar expression?

How can I write something new and unexpected?

Consider this issue in light of a favorite topic: food. The purpose of a dinner party isn't merely to sate your guests' hunger—they could easily go to the local greasy spoon for that—but rather to take them on a gastronomic journey. Certainly you want the food to taste good, but it's much more than that. You plan, prepare, and cook the food so that it has the proper texture, crunch, visual and flavorful variety. The spices should be in harmonious balance with each other. Writers know the same thing. If you want to make your writing memorable to readers, you must give them an aesthetic experience.

My colleague Dan Feigelson, author of *Practical Punctuation* (2008), talks about ebb and flow as essential components of any learning dynamic. Whenever we learn something new we begin by trying to educate ourselves (ebb): building awareness, absorbing information, taking a crash course on the subject. In time we find ourselves ready to apply (flow) what we have learned. As we'll see, both ebb and flow feature prominently in helping students gain mastery over these powerful pyrotechnics used by writers.

In this book we'll look at language play from various perspectives. Like the ripples created from a stone dropped in a pond, I'll start from the personal (my history, my own writing, writers I know) and then move outward to suggest ways we might apply these notions to the writing classroom, to better nourish the young writers who inhabit it.

2 *A Love Affair with Words*

Three-year-old girl on a tricycle,
talking to her father who is sitting on a park bench:

"You stay with your sun, Daddy. I'll ride with my wind."

I have always relished delicious language, surprising turns-of-phrase, words that are fun to say, or *le mot juste*: the right word at the right time. My fascination with words goes back to when I was a little boy and first realized that while *bare* and *bear* sound the same, they are two very different words.

In high school my best friend's father owned the *Oxford English Dictionary*, a two-volume behemoth so heavy it would break your foot if it fell on you. I was enthralled. I viewed that *OED* as a portal into a whole world I desperately wanted to be part of. A million pages . . . a gazillion words, each with its own secret history and various meanings. The *OED* featured a small drawer that, when slid open, revealed a special magnifying glass to help you investigate all those words. Holding that magnifying glass, I felt like a certified word-sleuth, armed and ready to start solving the mysteries of language.

Like most writers I know, I have always had an abiding interest in words for their own sake. Here's an excerpt from my book *Hello, Harvest Moon* (2003):

> *It floods the clam flats*
> *with lonely lunar light*
> *setting off an eruption of bubbles*
> *from crabs and clams tucked in mud.*

In a literal sense, the subject here is moonlight on a clam flat. But as much as anything these lines are about language itself—trying to put words together in such a way as to create fresh, musical sentences. You'll notice this preoccupation with language in nearly all my books.

* In *Fig Pudding* (1996) there is one chapter where the baby wants a "yidda yadda" for Christmas, and no one can figure out what he wants. Kids have told me that they enjoy this chapter, partly because they have their own younger sisters and brothers. They know that baby talk can be a distinct language with its own peculiar rules and hilarious grammatical structures.
* In *Marshfield Dreams* (2005a) one chapter is titled "Scuttlebutt," about a girl in my class who, much to my consternation, always seemed to know before I did when my mother was going to have another baby. Not only is *scuttlebutt* a fun word to say, but it plants a ludicrous image in the brain.
* In my novel *Flying Solo* (1998), a Hungarian storyteller named Klof Selat appears at a crucial juncture in the book. If you spell the name backward you get *folk tales*. I deliberately planted this inside joke, and readers never catch it. Never! Even so, I wouldn't consider it a failure—in fact, I'm glad I included it in the book.

Why do I play with language when I write?

* To give emphasis to a particular section of text
* To sharpen the meaning
* To create a surprise or unexpected effect
* To make one part sound more melodious
* To be playful for its own sake
* To be clever
* To inject a jolt of humor
* To be irreverent/subversive
* To keep my readers on their toes
* To keep myself alert

As with learning any new skill, language play requires deep, deliberate practice if you want to get good at it. Luckily, when I first looked for a place where I might start practicing, I didn't have to go far.

The Writer's Notebook

"My most important book is a book that has never been published, and never will be published," I tell students when I make an author visit to a school. After a suitable pause to build suspense, I ceremoniously unveil my writer's notebook while adding, "This is the book that feeds the ones that eventually get published."

Certainly the writer's notebook is a crucial part of what makes me a writer. This blank book provides an intimate, convenient place for collecting ideas, jotting down dreams, recording events, wondering, daydreaming, and reacting to the world. As I leaf through the various notebooks I have used over the past twenty years, I realize I have been using my writer's notebook as a laboratory for playing around with words, phrases, and expressions, plus collecting intriguing odds and ends of language I find lying around.

The Poetry of Everyday Talk

Keeping a writer's notebook is like dragging a wide net through the world; all kinds of squiggling creatures get snared in it. One of my favorite ways to use mine is to collect bits of talk I have overheard during the course of the day. One morning at an inservice workshop I heard one teacher remark to another: "This morning I was driving to school, but my car really wanted to go to Target."

When I mentioned to my teenage son that I often write down snippets of talk I overhear, Joseph was outraged.

"You mean you're spying on people!"

Well, yes. But not spying for any nefarious purpose. I have learned that people are at their most unguarded and revealing while they are engaged in casual talk. When I listen, I'm as much attuned to the flavor of this dialogue— the cadence, humor, local colloquialisms—as I am to the substance of what they are saying. Here are a few talk nuggets overheard and preserved in my notebook.

Overheard at a bar: *"Mothers raise their daughters and love their sons."*

My son Taylor (pointing): *"That car over there is a Chevy Lumina. Backwards, Lumina almost spells* animal, *but not quite. You don't know how much it bothers me that it doesn't."*

My brother Jim: *"A knife will cut you until it earns your respect."*

At night in bed my son Joseph, who is three, likes to "clip-on" (his words) to me, locking his arms and legs around my body while I read him his story. Last night when I put him to bed he protested: *"But Daddy, you didn't* story *me!"*

Overheard at Starbucks: *"Lemme tell you, my son was not a very good student. He graduated summa cum lucky."*

These examples all have surprise as a common denominator. Those moments when an unexpected phrase or a new use of a word (*story* as verb) makes us say "Ah!" constitute one of the central pleasures of language. Occasionally one of these nuggets finds its way into a published book. More often, however, I simply collect them like prized pieces of beach glass. And I use them for inspiration. Words such as these:

Artsy-fartsy	Gizmos	Prestidigitation
Boondoggle	Hanky-panky	Ricochet
Boychick	Impromptu	Rinky-dink
Calabash	Juggernaut	Sassafras
Cantankerous	Kerfuffle	Schnauzer
Cockamamie	Killjoy	Scuppernong
Contrapuntal	Lullabye	Succotash
Crescendo	Meshuggenah	Taboo
Dillydally	Nincompoop	Tchotchkes
Doodads	Obstreperous	Thingamajig
Flibbertigibbet	Panache	Thingamabob
Flummoxed	Persnickety	Topsy-turvy
Frolic	Phobophobia	Trifecta

Shimmering Sentences by Other Writers

Every writer hopes to inspire the reader, but where does a writer go for inspiration? I turn to other writers. I want a good story, sure enough, but I also seek books crammed with sentences that make me sit up and say, "Whoa! How the &#! did she do that?"

Whenever I come across a dazzling passage I make a habit of copying it into my writer's notebook, maybe hoping that in the act of copying it down my fingers might soak up some remnant of the original magic. I'm fascinated by writers who violate common ideas about usage, and get away with it. For instance, writers are advised not to be redundant by repeating a word, yet in this passage from *High Fidelity*, Nick Hornby does exactly that:

> *All we really had in common . . . was that we had been dumped by people, and that on the whole we were against dumping—we were fervent antidumpers. So how come I got dumped? (1995, 31)*

One of the hardest things in writing is to evoke a believable sense of place. Nobody does this better than Cormac McCarthy. Here's a passage from his novel *The Crossing*:

> *In the long steep light the raw umber mountains stood deeply shadowed in their folds and in the sky to the south a dozen buzzards turned in a slow crepe carousel. (1995, 212)*

The final image—the slow crepe carousel—took my breath away and sounds more like poetry than prose.

Another thing I noticed about McCarthy's novel: he certainly isn't shy about using (or even inventing) compound words. Often he strings a bunch of them together within a single sentence:

> *He halfhitched the catchrope to a fencepost. (57)*

Sometimes it's a single arresting image I'll encounter in a story or novel that makes its way into my notebook, like this one from *Three Junes* by Julia Glass:

> *Her shoulder was crazed with freckles. (2003, 4)*

I would never have thought to use *crazed* in this context, but then again, why not? An image like this encourages me to be looser and wilder when creating my own images. I'm drawn to places where the author tries strange or unusual imagery that doesn't seem as if it should work but somehow does, as in these two passages from *Girl, Interrupted* by Susanna Kaysen:

> *Lunatics are similar to designated hitters. Often an entire family is crazy, but since an entire family can't go into a hospital, one person is designated as crazy and goes inside. (1995, 95)*

And later in the same book:

> *The group [of patients] had an atomic structure: a nucleus of nuts surrounded by darting, nervous nurse-electrons charged with our protection. (48)*

For me, passages like these conjure up new possibilities of language. Like a sly crow who stashes sparkly tidbits in his nest, I pay homage to these writers by copying their words into my notebook. In this regard, my notebook becomes a pit stop where I can refuel and replenish my energy.

I use my notebook to observe and admire passages written by other writers, but it is also a safe place where I can play with language and try to bang together something the world has never seen before. Here are a few examples:

> *This sputtering, expensive pen is like a rich man who can't seem to clear his throat.*

> *a field of wildflowers—the Braille of bees*

> *Unfinished snow poem—*
> *   Whose idea was it to unroll*
> *   white carpets on the ground?*
> *   Or loose this swarm of wasps*
> *   to roam without a sound?*

During a recent visit to a local middle school, I talked to students about how I use my writer's notebook. The students, who had been keeping their own writer's notebooks, listened intently. One boy raised his hand.

"It sounds like your writer's notebook is where you do the rough drafts for your rough drafts," he observed thoughtfully.

"You're right." I paused a moment. "While I'm scribbling in my writer's notebook I sometimes feel like a mad scientist experimenting with words, altering, combining . . . and hoping nothing blows up!" (See figure.)

In *Holding On to Good Ideas in a Time of Bad Ones*, Tom Newkirk writes: "Teaching . . . is an ongoing series of microexperiments that extend and modify the repertoire of teachers. When we stop experimenting, we stop living as teachers" (2009, 31).

In this passage you could substitute *writer* or *writing* each time Newkirk used *teacher* or *teaching*. Writing, too, is an ongoing series of microexperiments. When we stop experimenting we stop living as writers. My writer's notebook is the primary place where I conduct these experiments. It is an insurance policy to prevent my writing from getting too staid, conventional, and predictable. It's an intimate personal space where I can:

* Hang out with my word brethren and sistren
* Reclaim my identity as a writer
* Improvise with sentences, even though I know many of those improvisations probably won't be successful and won't end up in a published piece of writing
* Do the regular work—oops, make that play—all writers must do in order to reinvent ourselves and our language

Putting the Writer's Notebook to Good Use

In the bibliography you'll find a list of published resources on the writer's notebook. I recommend Aimee Buckner's book *Notebook Know-How* (2005), which truly is a paragon of practicality.

Caution: the writer's notebook should be a free zone where students have carte blanche to collect, experiment, and play. If the notebook is going to have enduring value to your students, it is important that they feel as if they own it. Beware assigning students to use their notebooks for your own purposes. To the extent that the writer's notebook is perceived as a teacher thing (in control of the teacher), it will lose power for the students.

* Seek the notebook scribblings of writers known to your class, and share these examples with your students.
* Keep your own writer's notebook. Share appropriate excerpts with your students, especially examples involving playfulness with language.
* Encourage students, either individually or collectively, to start their own writer's notebooks. Make time for students to share with the class.
* In primary classrooms, consider having a class writer's notebook.
* Invite students to come up with their own metaphors for describing the writer's notebook. For example, Michael (a first grader) remarked to me, "Notebooks are . . . well, it's like you have sparks from a campfire that could start a fire. They haven't yet, but they could any time."

3

Writers Behaving Playfully

"Yokel," Shrek snapped.
"What have you in that pouch of yours?"
"Just some cold pheasant."
"Pheasant, peasant! What a pleasant present!"

William Steig, *Shrek!*

Writers from Homer to James Joyce to Virginia Woolf to e. e. cummings have created enduring works that explore themes of human existence: loss of innocence, illusions under which people live, the conflict between civilization and natural life, just to name a few. But the works of these authors also contain an astonishing cache of language play, some of which will make you laugh out loud. While reading Tom Robbins's novel *Even Cowgirls Get the Blues*, I came upon this section:

> *This sentence was made in Japan. This sentence glows in the dark. . . . This sentence has a crush on Norman Mailer. This sentence is a wino and doesn't care who knows it. Like many italic sentences, this one has Mafia connections. This sentence is a double Cancer with Pisces rising. This sentence lost its mind searching for the perfect paragraph. This sentence refuses to be diagramed. This sentence ran off with an adverbial clause. . . . This sentence can do the funky chicken. This sentence has seen too much and forgotten too little. This sentence is called "Speedo" but its real name is Mr. Earl. This sentence may be pregnant, it missed its period   This sentence suffered a split infinitive—and survived. . . . This sentence went to jail with Clifford Irving. This sentence went to Woodstock. And this little sentence went wee wee wee all the way home. (1990, 108)*

I love this passage. And I'm struck by what is *not* happening here. The author has stopped trying to develop his characters, describe the setting, move the narrative forward, or do any of the other things a novelist "should" be doing. Instead he has called a time-out, given himself permission to play with language, and we are richer for it.

The writing process movement had its genesis in a close look at how writers actually write. After studying the various ways writers rehearse, collect ideas, draft, revise, and so forth, educators like Donald Murray, Donald Graves, Peter Elbow, Lucy Calkins, Nancie Atwell, and others explored what implications these stages and strategies might have for the writing classroom.

To write this book I contacted a number of living writers, especially those whose works are read by children. I wanted to probe their attitudes toward language play. Do they use it in their writing? When I talked to Katherine Paterson, she pointed out the main character in *The Great Gilly Hopkins*, who is given to alliteration. Early in the novel we find Gilly speaking to a photograph of her mother.

> *I'd be good for you. You'd see. I'd change into a whole new person. I'd turn from gruesome Gilly into gorgeous, gracious, good, glorious Galadriel. And grateful. Oh, Courtney—oh, Mother, I'd be so grateful. (30)*

Dan Gutman is the author of the My Weird School Daze series. In these books the characters are constantly misinterpreting or mishearing words to comic effect. Here's an example from *Officer Spence Makes No Sense!*

> *"So what are you eating?" Michael asked Andrea. "Nuts and berries and veggies?"*
> *"My mom packed me some yummy tofu," Andrea told us.*
> **"TOE FOOD!"** *we all yelled.*
> *I'd rather die young than eat food made from toes.*
> *Andrea held up her fork with a piece of that toe food and stuff on it. It was white.*
> *Ugh! Disgusting! It looked like a big toe. I thought I was gonna throw up.*
> *"Not 'toe food,' dumbheads!" Andrea said. "It's tofu!"*
> *It sounded a lot like "toe food" to me.*

I asked Gutman why he uses wordplay in his books.

"I'm kinda fascinated by words that sound like other words," he told me. "When kids confuse one with the other, it can be hilarious. I like to use wordplay in My Weird School series for the simple reason that it's fun and silly, and I think kids like that."

Chris Crutcher is a young-adult novelist who has won several lifetime achievement awards. I experienced his love of wordplay firsthand when Chris, two other authors, and I were invited to speak to students at the Shanghai American School in China. At dinner one night, we had one savory dish we couldn't identify. Chris asked our host what it was.

"Bamboo," she explained.

"Bamboo," Chris repeated, shaking his head in amazement. "Shoot!"

When another author, Joel Schwartz, suggested we order the roast duck, Chris quickly retorted: "Only if you let me split the bill."

I mentioned to Chris that I notice a lot of wordplay in his novels.

"Mostly it's impulsive," he explained. "When I'm writing, my radar for words comes up."

I asked him to cite some favorite examples from his books.

"I have a character named TJ in *Whale Talk*," he said. "He was named by a hippie mother. His first name is Tao. He is later adopted by the Jones family. Tao Jones. In my novel *The Sledding Hill*, there is a fictional book being banned. Its title is the main character's name: Warren Peece. In *The Crazy Horse Electric Game*, one of the characters tells the story of a baseball catcher who plays naked. It's called 'The Catcher in the Raw.'"

I pointed out that many teenagers might not know what the Dow Jones refers to.

"True," Chris admitted, "but I throw in puns all the time solely for my own amusement. If I put a reference into a book, or a pun, I never expect all readers to get it. Most of the time it doesn't matter. If they don't get it, no harm done, go on with the story. If they do get it, it's a bonus for them and for me. With any luck, a story plays to all levels of reader. With puns in particular, if people get them it's cool, but if they don't, who cares? They don't even know you tried. In that regard they're all for the writer. But that's true of any 'voice' elements in writing."

Each writer I spoke to had a slightly different way of describing his or her penchant for playing with language.

"I think wordplay is a knee-jerk reaction for writers," Jane Yolen told me. "We are around words so much; they fascinate us, tease us, tickle us, and we respond."

I Stink! is a fabulous picture book about a garbage truck written by Kate McMullan (and illustrated by Jim McMullan). Kate enriches her story with a wealth of alliteration, onomatopoeia, and invented or distorted words such as *Mt. Trash-o-rama*.

"Why did you include all that marvelous wordplay?" I asked Kate.

"I just enjoy the process and don't really think about why," she told me. "No purpose, just an end in itself."

This response made me wonder if perhaps I was overthinking the whole issue. Maybe language play is so deeply ingrained in what writers do that it's almost biological; my question was like asking someone: Why do you breathe?

Language play is not a rare thing; in fact, it's so plentiful you can scarcely avoid it. You find it in conversation, pop songs, TV shows, advertisements, literature, greeting cards, brochures, magazines, and newspapers. On a recent morning I found these examples in the *Boston Globe* sports section:

This Is the Week to Tweak (winter football meetings)
Wright Can't Go Wrong Here (about the Pats' Mike Wright)
Good News on Injuries Comes Hand Over Foot (baseball)
Penguins March Slowed (hockey)

Here we encounter a catchy rhyme, a pun, an idiom, and an allusion to a film, all used in rapid succession. My friend Brock Dethier is head of the writing program at Utah State University. He is also a fine poet and songwriter.

"Why do you think writers play with words?" I asked him.

"Because it's fun!" he blurted out.

My first reaction was that fun seems like a frivolous goal. But maybe not. My research on boy writers has convinced me that *fun* is a Trojan horse for weightier educational terms like *ownership*, *engagement*, and *flow*. Fun matters. We have created this elaborate pedagogical contraption called the reading-writing workshop, but fun is the engine that makes it run.

It is true that language play creates a measure of fun for both the writer and the reader, but these pyrotechnics are more than self-indulgence, or frosting on the cake. Writers use them to create stronger, truer sentences. In this book we'll take a closer look at a range of powerful language pyrotechnics that every writer should have in his or her repertoire of crafting strategies.

"In all authors, deep down, there is a fear of banality," David Crystal writes in his book *Language Play*. "Of being accused of linguistic unoriginality. 'We've heard that before.' 'The language is full of clichés.' All authors try to avoid such charges by trying to be linguistically fresh. And the best way to do that is to bend and break the rules" (2006, 184).

Crystal is right. No writer or writing teacher can be satisfied with lackluster, formulaic sentences. If we aim to empower young writers, we must encourage them to explore the limitless possibilities and effects with words that are readily available to us all.

Lessons from a Talking Elf

I'd like to sue ya, but I'd have to get a lawya!

Robert, age 6

I have learned about language play by listening to everyday conversation, by admiring it in books written by other writers, and by experimenting with it myself in my writer's notebook. But nobody has taught me more about it than my son Robert. I had a front row seat to observe and enjoy all the ways he used language from the time he first began making grunts and exclamations, seedling sounds that quickly sprouted into deliberate speech.

Robert's oral language took flight around the age of six or seven months, and he has been airborne ever since. Here are some snippets of his talk, preserved in my writer's notebook.

Robert (2½) is keenly aware that JoAnn is pregnant. This morning I catch him pulling a pair of pliers from my toolbox.

"I need a big wrench," he says earnestly, *"so I can open the door in Mommy's bottom to let the baby come out."*

Robert has trouble using negative constructions in a sentence. His pre-school teacher reports that Robert will often say, *"This is the biggest balloon I never saw!"* Or, *"You're the best friend I never had."*

Robert has a terrible sore throat that lasted three long days. Finally his throat improves enough for him to eat without pain. I take him to a restaurant for breakfast, and he carefully eats a bagel.

"How's your sore throat?" I ask him.

"It hopped away."

Robert puts three small toy trucks into a glass canning jar. He screws on the top and peers in, grinning.
"They're all glassed up!"

Robert (3) has morphed into a monster lately. He delights in saying shocking things just to see how we will respond.
"I feel happy when cars hit people," he announces. Or, "You're dumb, Daddy." Then he sits, blinking, calmly awaiting my reaction.

At the town pool Robert throws sand on the back of Josh, his best friend. Soon he's dumping it on Josh's head.
"Stop that!" I tell him.
"I love Josh," Robert says by way of defending himself. Smiling at Josh, he murmurs, "You're awesome, Josh."
Then he tells me confidentially, "Awesome means: you're dumb."

Robert pushes his arms through the sleeves of his T-shirt:
"These are smooth roads!"

Robert beams at his little brother, Joseph, *"I don't like your head, but I like you!"*

This morning I kneel in front of Robert, helping him put on his boots. Tenderly, he caresses the bald part of my head: *"It's like the sun breaking through the clouds!"*

Robert (4): *"Reuben is a real paint in the neck."*

On a family trip to Shelter Island I showed Robert a razor clam.
"But I want to find laser clams. They shoot people with lasers."

Robert (4) loves words: *"My favorite words are flip trick and sweet treat."*

He has a computer program that makes colorful designs. We don't have a color printer, so he can't print it out.

"It's really a shame we don't have a color printer, Daddy."

Then he smiles and motions at his little brother. *"If Joseph said* shame, *wouldn't that be a strong word?"*

Robert has lately become obsessed with farts. He concocts his own version of "The Little Drummer Boy": *"Mary farted, ba rump pa bum bum . . ."*

His preschool class has a safety lesson about what to do if your clothes ever catch on fire.

"You're supposed to stop, drop, and fart," he explains.

JoAnn drinks her coffee with milk; I add milk plus sugar. Robert likes to sneak a sip of mine: *"I love Daddy's candy coffee."*

Today Robert sent Joseph into paroxysms of laughter by telling him a story he invented: "The Legend of Butt Crack Man."

Robert is in first grade. When we move to Alabama, he is told he must answer questions from adults with either *"Yes, sir"* or *"Yes, ma'am."* But Robert finds a subversive way around this problem.

"Robert, please pick up your toys," I tell him.

Smiling: *"Yes, ma'am."*

After supper I suggest he work on his homework.

Smirking: *"Yes, Ma'amster."*

Next night JoAnn says, *"Robert, please set the table for supper."*

"Yes, Ma'amsteration Constipation."

As Robert grew older he continued to delight us with his language. On ski trips he would start talking the moment we got into the car and wouldn't stop until we arrived at the mountain hours later. Today, as a college student, Robert has developed into a fluent, confident writer. He writes poetry as well as rap lyrics that "play with the rhythms in words," as he explains it.

As I reread these notebook entries, it's tempting to take these verbal riches and sort them into categories—a playful rhyme, an invented word, a striking image, a wacky metaphor, and so forth—though Robert certainly wasn't thinking of categories when he used them. I envision his language as a mass of fertile seaweed, ragged but interconnected, a big chunk of unkempt kelp. We might lean in for a closer look, but we should be wary of dissecting it, and never forget that it constitutes the whole language of one child.

Surely, one boy does not a scientific study make, but if I had to extract any lessons from all this, three things stand out.

1. The importance of talk. Long before I saw any evidence of wordplay in Robert's writing, I observed it in his oral language. Too often talk is the forgotten stepchild when it comes to learning, but we neglect it at our peril. Talk is the medium in which kids first get comfortable playing with words, allowing a hundred quick drafts and revisions. When it comes to wordplay, talk is like one of those Etch A Sketches; they can try it, quickly erase, and try it again.

2. A willingness to bend/break the rules of language. Robert never hesitated to alter a word or phrase to suit his purpose, even if it meant violating a particular convention of grammar.

3. The presence of humor. While it is tempting to dismiss humor as a silly side-show, it is also undeniably true that humor is woven into almost every one of these examples. How can it not be one of the essential ingredients?

Set against the stark backdrop of tests and standards, Robert's language play may seem charming but irreverent. But in the world of our family it had real value.

*   It gave us concrete evidence that he was growing into a stronger, more confident language user.
*   It provided countless language stories we knew would be treasured by relatives and friends.
*   It cracked us up. Hey, don't knock it; on many stressful days when JoAnn or I sorely needed a belly laugh, one of his zany one-liners did the trick.

Robert probably was born with a natural verbal aptitude that would one day carry over into his facility with writing. But it's limiting to consider language play something you either have or don't have, like the ability to roll your tongue. I believe that this kind of play is something all of us can become better at. And you become more skillful not merely through work and study, but through play.

5 A Developmental Perspective

Children . . . grow up within a world of language play.
It permeates their lives. It is their main means of
achieving rapport with their parents and peers.

David Crystal, *Language Play*

How do we encourage language play in children? Most parents have never had to ponder this question because doing so is almost instinctive. When Robert was little we read him stories and nursery rhymes, concocted rhymes in the bath, played games that were silly and tactile ("This little piggy went to market . . ."). When Robert initiated pretend games ("Play puppy with me!") we patiently got down on our knees to play along. Like most children he adored songs, especially those that mangled words or rearranged the syllables in some convoluted way:

> *Robert, Robert, bo-bobert,*
> *Banana-fana-fo-fobert*
> *Fee, fie, mo-mobert,*
> *Robert!*
> *Taylor, Taylor, bo-baylor,*
> *Banana-fana-fo-faylor . . .*

Parents might righteously assert that we do such things to "promote the language development" of our children, or some other highfalutin purpose, though I suspect it's much simpler than that. Mostly we do so because it's patently clear that kids love it, and because our own parents played similar word games with us when we were small.

In his book *Language Play* (1998), David Crystal points out that during the first year of a child's life ninety percent of what parents say to a child is playful and fun. Ninety percent! These playful language experiences dwarf all those instances of serious speech, occasions when a parent might say, "Stay away from the fireplace" or, "Eat your cereal."

Picture a mother singing to a three-year-old: "Mairzy doats and dozy doats and liddle lamzy divey, a kiddley divey too, wouldn't you?" The child begs her mother to sing it again and again. It's not the meaning of the song but rather the delicious sounds, rhymes, and rhythms that the girl finds so irresistible.

Many researchers have documented what parents observe with their own eyes: how children continue to delight in language play throughout the preschool years.

* Catherine Garvey, a child-language researcher, watched one three-year-old spend nearly fifteen minutes taking apart and varying the syllable structure of the word yesterday. (Crystal 1998, 166)
* James Britton (1970) tells the story of a small boy brought to a conference, who went dancing through the hall chanting repeatedly the phrase maximum capacity. (Crystal 1998, 166)
* My sister Elaine recalls how her daughter adored games that involved pretending: "Rebecca loved to star in her stories. She loved being Cinderella and having me order her to work or tell her she couldn't go to the ball."

Adults universally cherish the verbal antics of young children, even when the language play is accidental. One day, when Joseph was four years old, he innocently asked: "Daddy, could you really get in a barrel and go over Viagra Falls?"

Art Linkletter made a career out of the hilarious ways children use language; he discovered that adults find enduring value in sentences that are not correct or conventional. This is universally true in most of the adults I know. Late one morning a friend of mine found her son in the bathroom, sitting on the potty.

"But you already did your poops," she pointed out.

"I know, but I'm crap-ticing," he solemnly explained.

Erica Pecorale, who teaches at Long Island University, remembers the time a first grader explained to her that there are two Aprils.

"There is April the month," he said. "And there is April Ham Lincoln."

Another time the same boy confided to her: "Did you know there are two Phillips? There's the name Phillip, and then when you go to the gas station and say: 'Can you please fill-up the tank?'"

Language stories like this one become almost sacred, told and retold until they become a permanent part of family lore. While diligent parents may choose to correct a child's misuse of a word or phrase, at the same time we cherish the intelligence behind these "errors" and the stunning freshness created when the child invents a new word, or novel usage of a word.

In *The Muses Among Us: Eloquent Listening and Other Pleasures of the Writer's Craft*, Kim Stafford reveals how his father created a family book to collect the sparkling gems spoken by his four children.

> *My parents called it* Lost Words, *and it was a compendium of the unusual things the four children in my family said when we were small, before we went to school. Both our parents were teachers, especially alert to adventures in language. And in his own daily writing practice, my father wrote down his favorites from our random utterance, and then he compiled them into a little book. This book is important not because it is unusually brilliant. Every child I have met has unique insights and ways of expressing them. But* Lost Words *was our book. The ideas between its covers were our own philosophic landscape, and the language was our collective creation. My brother, Bret, my sisters, Kit and Barbara, and I together challenged each other to figure out the world, sentence by sentence, and question by question. Just because our parents were the teachers in the family did not mean we weren't all thinkers, writers, makers of culture. In* Lost Words, *democratic inclusion started in the family and became my career. (2003, 107; the entire chapter, with excerpts from* Lost Words, *can be found in Appendix E.)*

To summarize, children love wordplay and show an affinity for it. You might say that their brains are wired for playing with language. The child who engages in wordplay learns at an early age that:

* Words and sentences are as malleable as play dough. Rules are meant to be broken. You can pretty much do whatever you want.

* Reading, singing, and chanting are pleasurable activities. For this reason, children will happily practice a song or poem again and again until they master it.
* Wordplay creates rapport between those who use it. A child singing "Skinna marinky dinky dink, skinna marinky doo" with a babysitter, grandmother, or big brother develops a closer bond with that person.

In addition, language play carries the huge cognitive benefit of helping children become more proficient language users. Many educators have pointed this out, including Vygotsky, who famously described a child's language as "a head taller" during play. Jerome Bruner said that "language is most daring and most advanced when it is used in a playful setting" (1984, 196).

David Crystal argues that playing with language is a sophisticated endeavor because knowing how to break a rule requires you to understand the rule in the first place.

"To play with language requires that . . . a person has sensed what is normal and is prepared to deviate from it," he says. "Language players are in effect operating within two linguistic worlds at once, the normal and the abnormal, and trading them off against each other. It seems very likely that, the greater our ability to play with language, the more we will reinforce our general development of metalinguistic skills" (1998, 181). Crystal goes on to say that language play "becomes a bridge between the familiar and the unfamiliar linguistic worlds. Manipulating structure brings . . . an increased awareness of the way language works" (187).

Most children arrive at school with a wealth of language play in their experience: songs, riddles, jokes, nursery rhymes, verbal rituals, and games. They already know that playing with words is a blast.

"When a child arrives in school, his linguistic life has been one willingly given over to language play," Crystal says. "From a child's point of view, language play must be what language is chiefly for. Then they arrive in school. Where language play has traditionally been frowned upon" (183).

In a classroom setting, the tenor of language play often feels dramatically different from what the child has ever known before. There's far less play and laughter in many classrooms. Instead of being woven into rich stories and songs, words are often decontextualized, pulled from living texts and studied in isolation.

"It seems that the study of words has become *only* about reading and vocabulary knowledge," Franki Sibberson, author of *Beyond Leveled Books*, noted in an interview with me. "In school, we have taken it and shrunk it down to mean nothing more than that. We have lost the study of and thinking about words as readers and writers."

Face it: we live in tense times. Speakers carefully parse their language, rereading speeches three or four times to make sure their words won't be misconstrued. People are terrified of offending anybody. Teachers, who live under the watchful eyes of parents and administrators, feel particularly vulnerable in this regard. Nowadays even a relatively mild word like *hell* in a novel would make many teachers uneasy and gun-shy.

Language play pulls in the other direction. It subverts the dominant paradigm. Refusing to stay on the walkway, it romps through the lush and forbidden grass. It disputes the fundamental notion that there is a right way and a wrong way to use a word. Furthermore, it challenges the basic teacher-to-student flow of information by acknowledging the reality that often our students know more about language than we do.

I propose a toast. I say let's usher in an era of glasnost for language play. I suggest we open the windows, take a fresh look at all the pyrotechnics that writers use on a regular basis, and see what implications they have for the writing classroom. In the next five chapters we'll take a closer look at particular kinds of language play that are useful to writers. We may have to dodge a few patches of quicksand here and there, but I think we'll find that the payoffs far outweigh the risks.

GETTING SERIOUS

Inventing Words

O frabjous day! Callooh! Callay!

Lewis Carroll, "Jabberwocky"

Our friend Stephanie stopped by with Daniel, a rambunctious two-year-old. He gobbled down the cookie I offered him and held out his hand for another. When Dan saw my son Adam drinking a glass of water, he impulsively reached for it. But Adam held on to his glass.

"I don't blame you," Stephanie told Adam. "After Daniel finishes drinking, you'll have lots of little floaties in your glass."

Context really is everything. *Floaties* may not be an actual word, yet as soon as Stephanie uttered it, everybody knew what it meant.

If you view language as something fixed and permanent like the periodic table of elements or the laws of Newtonian physics, you might not have much patience with the notion that words can be invented. In this chapter I'll argue that the English language is not fixed but dynamic, a language that continues to evolve on a daily basis. In this context, the invention of words makes perfect sense and should be welcomed in the classroom, not discouraged.

Alpha Centauri is the closest star system to our solar system, a mere 4.37 light-years away. Astronomers didn't invent Alpha Centauri—it was out there for billions of years until astronomers stumbled onto its existence. But the origin of stars is notably different from the origin of words. Words were created by people; many have been invented by authors. William Shakespeare is credited with having invented over 1,000 words that are now full-fledged members of the English language, including *amazement, dishearten, dwindle, entomb, cold-blooded, deafening, gossip, hoodwink, moonbeam, torture, tranquil,* and *zany.* He also made up hundreds of other words that never became part of regular English usage, clunkers that include *unhair* and *annexment* (Bryson 1990, 64).

Inventing words is a phenomenon that continues today. Every year new words get added to the English language. Recent inductees include *aerobicize, mentee, blowback, ponzu, netroots, malware,* and *subprime.*

The word *snafu* was created during World War Two and is an acronym for *situation normal all fouled up. Stick-to-itiveness* (the ability to stay with a project and see it through to completion) is older, dating back to 1867. I came upon a similar word in a *New Yorker* column written by Malcolm Gladwell, "Most Likely to Succeed," a fascinating article about the difficulty in predicting whether or not a person will become an exceptional teacher. Gladwell writes:

> *[Jacob] Kounin called that ability "withitness," which he defined as 'a teacher's communicating to the children by her actual behavior (rather than by verbally announcing: 'I know what's going on') that she knows what the children are doing, or has the proverbial 'eyes in the back of her head.'" It stands to reason that to be a great teacher you have to have withitness. But how do you know whether someone has withitness until she stands up in front of a classroom of twenty-five wiggly Janes, Lucys, Johns, and Roberts and tries to impose order? (December 15, 2008)*

Children's literature has traditionally been one of the most fertile breeding grounds when it comes to inventing words. The verbs *chortle, burble,* and *galumph* were originally nonsense words in Lewis Carroll's "Jabberwocky" (2000). Eventually they worked their way into everyday use. Roald Dahl originated many new words, including *rubbsquash* and *snozzcumber* in *The BFG,* and *hornswogglers, snozzwangers,* and *whangdoodles* in *Charlie and the Chocolate Factory.*

In *Mrs. Dole Is Out of Control!,* the first book of Dan Gutman's My Weird School Daze series, we find this sentence: "Remember the time we had a food fight in the vomitorium?" As with *floaties,* the meaning of *vomitorium* is all too clear.

Poet Betsy Franco wrote a poem titled "Symmetricats" (see figure on page 36). I asked Betsy how she came up with that word. Did she start with the theme of the collection (cats), or did the poem originate from the word *symmetrical*?

"My friend had two cats who always sat symmetrically," Betsy explained. "As soon as I realized what they were doing, the word *symmetricats* came to my mind."

"Symmetricats" by Betsy Franco

Sniglets and Wanted Words

A neologism (from Greek *neo* = "new" + *logos* = "word") is defined as a relatively recently devised word or phrase that has not been accepted into mainstream usage. The online Urban Dictionary (www.urbandictionary.com) contains hundreds of comical neologisms, including *musquirt*, which is defined as the runny liquid substance that comes out of the mustard bottle before the actual mustard if you don't shake it well before use. (Others have insisted that this liquid should be called *bottlejuice*.)

One example of a neologism, invented by comedian Rich Hall, is the *sniglet*, which he defined as "any word that doesn't appear in the dictionary, but should." Some examples include:

Foodgitives: the food on one side of a TV dinner tray that escapes to the other side

Furnidents: the indentations left in carpet after moving heavy furniture

Glackett: the ball inside a can of spray paint or other aerosol can for stirring the contents inside the can

Fenderberg: the chunk of ice that builds up behind your wheel in winter

Googlegänger: a person with your name who shows up when you Google yourself

Execuglide: the act of using your wheeled office chair to move from one side of the office to another

Toastaphobia: the fear of sticking a fork into a toaster even when it's unplugged

Timefoolery: setting the alarm clock ahead of the real time in order to fool yourself into thinking you are not getting up so early (Hall 1985)

I learned that Hall created the word *perdiddel* to describe a car with only one working headlight. This surprised me because *perdiddel* was a working part of our family's lexicon twenty years ago, long before I knew what a sniglet was. Our kids made a game out of seeing who could be the first to spot a perdiddel whenever we went out for a family drive. We had several other related words:

*   Collywobble: car with one of the small front lights out
*   Dimdiddle: car with one headlight dimmed

Barbara Wallraff explores the concept of invented words in her book *Word Fugitives: In Pursuit of Wanted Words* (2006). Wallraff devises a number of necessary words that should exist but don't:

Q: What's the word for that restless feeling that causes me to peer into the refrigerator when I'm bored?

A: *Fridgety.*

Q: What's the word for one's offspring when they become adults?

A: *Offsprung* (or maybe *Unchildren*).

Wallraff suggests *guestlessness* as the word for the irrational fear you have when throwing a party and you're worried that no one will show up.

There's a long tradition of inventing words in the world of advertising, where they are known as "coined words." To help sell Smarties candy, for example, some clever soul invented the word *WotalotIgot!*

English is not a static subject but rather a restless organism that ebbs, flows, and pulsates. Our language is generative, a fertile lake continuously being fed by everyday people and current events. While some invented words are no more than arcane curiosities, others eventually become respectable members of the language. Only time will tell which is which. Even if a word never makes it into the dictionary, it serves a legitimate purpose to the person who uses it.

Slang and Jargon

I was riding on the Loon Mountain gondola with my son Joseph when he pointed out a young skier barreling down the slope.

"Watch this kid, Dad," Joseph said. "He's wicked steeze."

"Steeze?" I repeated. "Huh?"

Joseph rolled his eyes. "C'mon, Dad, get with it! *Steeze* is a combination of style and ease."

Steeze is an example of slang, which is a hotbed for all manner of language play. Dictionary.com defines *slang* as "very informal usage in vocabulary and idiom that is characteristically more playful, metaphorical, elliptical, vivid, and ephemeral than ordinary language."

To adult ears slang often sounds irreverent if not inappropriate. But being disrespectful is not the point. The chief use of slang is to show you're one of the gang. *Slang* has a twin, *jargon*, which is defined as the specialized vocabulary peculiar to a particular trade, profession, or group. For instance, here is some jargon from the publishing world:

F&Gs: folded and gathered sheets of a book that are often sent out for review

Stet: proofreading mark on a copyedited manuscript that means "leave as originally written"

Widow: a single word or short line at the top of a page in a book; widows are to be avoided

Orphan: unpublished manuscript left behind when the acquiring editor moves to a different publishing house

Recently one of my editors returned to me all the stuff (sketches, galleys, manuscript, etc.) that was used in making my picture book *Twilight Comes Twice* (1997b). I learned that this material is commonly known as *dead matter*.

Every profession has its own particular jargon, which is often unintelligible to people who are not in the group. Once upon a time I worked in the travel business where the jargon included:

Pax: passengers
Stags: single men on a vacation
Hots and colds: hors d'oeuvres at a cocktail reception
No-shows: passengers who don't show up for a trip
Plus plus: tax and gratuity added to a restaurant bill

Slang and *jargon* would seem to be twins, or at least siblings, yet adults tend to respond to them very differently, being suspicious of one while respectful of the other. But perhaps they are not so different. Like jargon, slang signals membership in a group. We might think of slang as the jargon of youth. It would be interesting to invite young writers to gather the jargon from worlds they are familiar with: camp, Scouting, sports activities, even their parents' professions.

When Kids Invent Words

Rebecca Shoniker, a literacy coach in North Carolina, visited a second-grade class that had been reading *Frindle* by Andrew Clements, a book in which one boy invents a new word (*frindle*) for pen.

"I got an idea," one boy said after they finished reading the book. "Maybe we could try to make our own worminations."

"What do you mean?" Rebecca asked.

"A wormination," he explained, "is what you get when you combine two words."

Once again, this anecdote puts forth the importance of talk. If you want to see kids inventing words, tune in to their everyday speech because that's where kids have the requisite comfort level to test-drive their newest concoctions.

One morning I made breakfast for my son Joseph, who was four. I cut a slice of cantaloupe, scooped out the seeds, removed the melon from the rind, and put the slice on a plate. But Joseph just sat there, lower lip extended unhappily.

"What's wrong?" I asked.

He pointed to the melon. "It's all gloomy."

"Gloomy?"

I leaned in to take a closer look. The seeds were gone, but the top of the slice had a loose, gelatinous quality.

"I can't eat that gloomy part," Joseph said.

"But that's the best part," I argued. "It's very sweet."

He frowned. "It's very gloomy."

Sighing, I got a knife and removed the top eighth of an inch. Finally he started to eat. In my family we still refer to the *gloomy* part of the melon.

Some kids remove a toy from its box and play with it pretty much as suggested by the instructions. Others immediately start changing it around, tailoring the toy to their own purposes. When it came to words, my son Robert would fall into the second category. I remember one morning when his allergies were acting up. I could hear him sneezing at his computer.

"You sound terrible," I said.

"Yeah, I'm struggling," he admitted, loudly blowing his nose.

Not long after that, I overheard Robert talking about a family he knew.

"Yeah, they're all strugglers. Nothing comes easy for any of them." He thought for a moment, and laughed. "Come to think of it, even the dog is a struggler!"

A bit later, Robert's friend Trey came down with a bad case of the flu. Robert told me, "Trey's really got the strugs."

During his senior year of high school Robert went on a foreign study program to Spain. He was supposed to come back home in late January, but JoAnn suggested he return a week earlier.

"Yeah, okay," Robert agreed. "I think the last week here is just going to be strugglesome anyways."

I was struck by the ease with which Robert fluidly changed the word to suit his purpose. *Struggle* (a verb) and *struggling* (adjective) soon morphed into *a struggler* or *the strugs* (nouns), or *strugglesome* (a new adjective that is still used by his friends). Robert treated *struggle* as a "pet word"—feeding it, enjoying it, and also training it to do this trick or that.

Bringing It to the Writing Workshop

In Chapter 16 you'll find several craft lessons designed to encourage young writers to invent words. Craft lessons like these send an unambiguous signal to students that the writing workshop is a laboratory for playing with words.

Craft Lessons: Inventing Words
Inventing Words (K–2), page 106
Inventing Words (3–4), page 115
Inventing Words (5+), page 122

Related Children's Books
* *Once Upon a Twice* by Denise Doyen (see Appendix G for the first two pages of text). This picture book contains a wealth of invented words—*preycautions, mouncelors*—that will provoke lively class discussion as to how and why the author created them.
* *Frindle* by Andrew Clements. This beloved novel tells the story of a boy who invents a new word—*frindle*—for pen, and then succeeds in getting the whole school to use this invented word.
* The Harry Potter series. In order to write these books, J. K. Rowling had to create myriad new words, including *Quidditch, muggle, Horcrux*, and *butterbeer*, just to name a few.
* Books by Dr. Seuss, especially *The Sneetches and Other Stories*.

Seth Loomis, a fifth grader in Georgetown, Massachusetts, is the author of "Getting Phoo Dog" (see Appendix F). It's apparent from the very first sentence that Seth is a strong writer. In the second-to-last paragraph he uses the word *confuzzled*, a hybrid of *confused* and *puzzled*.

"*Confuzzled* is a word but most dictionaries don't have it," Seth told me. "When you type it in, most computers do not think it is a word."

Skilled carpenters, mechanics, and surgeons are constantly faced with situations that force them to improvise or jury-rig a solution to a thorny problem. In a similar way, Seth's use of this word *confuzzled* shows a flexible writer with a willingness to create a word when the right one does not exist. In some schools *confuzzled* would be circled and marked wrong. To me, it is one of the best things about this piece. The word demonstrates a confident writer in full control of his language. What more could we want for our young writers?

Creating new words may sound like a rather far-fetched notion, but in fact it is a deliberate strategy used by our most skilled authors. For example, Jerry Spinelli's novel *Maniac Magee* contains this sentence: "One morning in early July, cruising down the appleskin hour, Maniac thought he heard footsteps other than his own."

At another point in that book we encounter a character named Mars Bar who walks with a "super-slow dip-stride slumpshuffle," which is said to stop traffic because it takes him so long to cross the street. I asked Spinelli to share his thoughts about inventing words like *appleskin* and *slumpshuffle*.

"There's no reason to believe there's a perfect word waiting for every storytelling need," Spinelli replied. "When the occasion arises and the right word isn't in the dictionary, make one up. We custom-make suits and chili and tricked-out cars—so why not words?"

7

Puns

**Hanging is too good for a man who makes puns;
he should be drawn and quoted.**

Fred Allen

A pun is a phrase that deliberately exploits confusion between similar-sounding words or a word with two meanings, often for humorous effect:

> *Atheism* is a *non-prophet* institution.
> Someone's *karma* ran over my *dogma*.
> A vulture boards a plane, carrying two dead *possums*. The attendant looks at him and says, "I'm sorry, sir, only one *carrion* allowed per passenger."

Puns reveal language at its most pliable, able to occupy two spaces at the same time. This duality is an essential element of play itself. A father plays "Shark" in the pool with his toddler, who squeals in horror and delight, enthralled with this powerful creature who can be a dangerous shark but also a reassuring father all at the same time.

Puns are the lowest kind of wit, or the highest, depending on your perspective. We may think of puns and double meanings as rarefied wordplay for extremely clever people; in fact, our language is rife with them.

Puns in Everyday Life

Recently I visited Dr. Wittner, my wonderful seventy-year-old dentist. While he was in the process of fitting me for a crown, Dr. Wittner put in soft plastic foam and held it in my mouth for a minute. When it had sufficiently solidified, he pulled it out and examined it.

"There. You made a good impression."

Later that same day, while I was on an elevator, a man pushed the button for the lobby.

"I would hate to work as an elevator man," he remarked to me. "That job would be so depressing."

He grinned; I groaned. Have you ever noticed that while other people's puns make us groan, our own puns always strike us as brilliant?

In chess, you can "fork" an opponent by threatening two pieces at the same time—for instance, moving your knight so that it puts the other player's king in check while simultaneously imperiling his queen. This devastating tactic can be ruinous to your opponent. A pun works in a similar manner: it slyly occupies two spaces at the same time. In doing so, it demonstrates a facet of language both supple and surprising. In this chapter we'll touch on where puns can be found, various kinds of puns, and how we might introduce this concept to young writers.

In Journalism

Pick up any newspaper or magazine, and if you don't stumble over a half dozen puns, well, you need a stronger cup of coffee. Headline writers are particularly fond of them.

> Humorists Say Every Pun Is Its Own Re-Word
> Phoenix Suns Rising in the West
> Collectors Troll Internet for Rare Figurines [wizards and trolls]

Sports journalism has always been fertile ground for language play in general and puns in particular. While I was in New York City recently, I picked up a copy of the *New York Post*. In the sports section I found an article about Yankees pitcher Andy Pettitte. Pettitte misjudged the market for free-agent pitchers and turned down the Yankees' offer of $10 million for the 2009 season. When the free-agent market crashed, along with athletes' salaries, the Yankees lowered their offer and Pettitte was forced to sign a contract for a mere $5.5 million, poor guy. The headline for the *Post* article made me both wince and chuckle: "Andy Learns 'Lessen'" (January 27, 2009).

In Advertising

When it comes to embedding a slogan into the mind of a consumer, nothing works better than a pun. Advertisers have used them in countless ad campaigns.

Morton salt: *When it rains, it pours.*
Michelin tires: *When it pours, it reigns.*
Pioneer stereo: *Everything you hear is true.*
Range Rover: *It's how the smooth take the rough.*
Lea & Perrins: *The Worcester Saucerer.*
Frosted Chex: *Chexellent or what?*
IBM: *I think, therefore IBM.*
John Deere tractors: *Nothing runs like a Deere.*

We may not admire the world of advertising but we must admit that this a real-world genre kids know and are interested in. One way to attune students' ears to puns is to invite them to look for puns in TV commercials and other advertisements. Make time for students to share the ones they find.

In Literature

Puns occupy a long and distinguished place in literature. Oscar Wilde was famous for his facility with puns and clever one-liners: "Immanuel isn't a pun, he Kant be!"

In Lewis Carroll's *Alice's Adventures in Wonderland* we find this passage:

"And how many hours a day did you do lessons?" said Alice, in a hurry to change the subject.
"Ten hours the first day," said the Mock Turtle: "nine the next, and so on."
"What a curious plan!" exclaimed Alice.
"That's the reason they're called lessons," the Gryphon remarked: "because they lessen from day to day."

While most literary heavyweights tapped into the power of puns, nobody could equal William Shakespeare.

"Shakespeare so loved puns that he put 3,000 of them—that's right, 3,000—into his plays," notes Bill Bryson in his book *The Mother Tongue*, "even to the extent of inserting them in the most seemingly inappropriate places, as when in *King Henry IV*, Part 1, the father of Hotspur learns of his son's tragic death and remarks that Hotspur is now Coldspur" (1990, 228).

Pun-derful Jokes

Q: What kind of shoes are made from banana skins?
A: *Slippers.*

Q: How do you know if it's raining cats and dogs?
A: *When you step in a poodle.*

Flip through any collection of jokes for kids and you'll find countless jokes like these, most of them playing off the way words imitate the sounds of other words.

Knock knock.
Who's there?
Dwayne.
Dwayne who?
Dwain the bathtub, I'm dwounin'!

Q: What kind of bee lives in a graveyard?
A: *A zom—bee.*

Kids universally adore such jokes, though you wouldn't necessarily know it by watching them.

"If humor is to be judged by how much laughter [a joke] generates, then what we have here is not humor, for laughter is conspicuous for its absence," notes David Crystal. "Rarely does even the flicker of a smile cross the children's faces. . . .

Enjoyment, rather than humor, is what language play is chiefly about" (1998, 16).

Many teachers write wordplay jokes on the board for students to read when they walk into class each morning. Kids will read and reread them, vetting the words for possible double meanings, because everyone wants to be in on the humor.

The "Tom Swifty" is an intriguing subcategory of puns that will appeal to middle school and secondary students. The name comes from the Tom Swift adventure novels.

"I need a pencil sharpener," Tom said *bluntly*.
"Your fly is open," was Tom's *zippy* reply.

The key word in a Tom Swifty is the adverb, adjective, or verb that both properly and punningly refers to what the sentence is about.

"The doctor had to remove my left ventricle," Tom said *half-heartedly*.
"Let's dig up the bodies," Bill said *gravely*.
"We must hurry," said Tom *swiftly*.
"I only have clubs, diamonds, and spades," Tom said *heartlessly*.
"I don't like hot dogs," Sam said *frankly*.
"Take the prisoner downstairs," Phil said *condescendingly*.
"Drop the gun," Dave said with a *disarming* smile.
"I lost my hair," Jacob *bawled*.
 "You can't have any of my oysters," Tom said *shellfishly*.

As you can see, Tom Swifties are marked by gallows humor—this fact alone virtually guarantees their appeal to older children.

Double Meanings

One form of the pun is the double meaning: a word or expression used in a given context so that it can be understood in two ways. A recent article in the *Boston Globe* was titled: "Fake Wrestlers Pinned Down by State Regulations." The double meaning is a two-for-one bonus deal, a buy-one-get-one-free, as the reader is presented simultaneously with both the figurative and the literal meaning of a phrase like "pinned down." Double meaning makes the piece more interesting, adding resonance and sly humor. But a double meaning can also add depth to a serious piece.

Rick Reilly writes on sports for *Sports Illustrated*. One of my favorite Reilly pieces is "Flying in the Face of Reason" (see Appendix H), which explores the tragic plane crash involving the Oklahoma State basketball team. The team flew in two small planes during a snowstorm, one of which crashed, killing all the passengers on that plane. Coach Eddie Sutton must live with the knowledge that he was the one who decided which players flew on which plane. My favorite sentence in Reilly's article is the very last one, which can be read in two ways, and braids together the two themes of the piece, basketball and grief:

> *All three planes made it safely to Lincoln, where the Cowboys lost to Nebraska 78–75 in overtime.*
> *The newspaper said they had trouble rebounding.*

A double meaning could be described in musical terms. You can play separate piano notes to make a melody. But you can also play two or three notes at the same time to produce a chord. Like a musical chord, a double meaning puts forth simultaneous meanings that can blend together to create a unique kind of beauty.

Bringing It to the Writing Workshop

Chapter 16 includes several craft lessons designed to help you bring the concept of puns into your classroom:

Craft Lessons: Puns

Related Children's Books

* Poetry from J. Patrick Lewis (examples can be found in Appendix I). These short, punchy poems allow young readers to quickly glean the gist of the pun.

* *Punished!* by David Lubar is a short, easy-to-read chapter book, and one I highly recommend to help kids get a feel for what puns are and how they work. At the beginning of the book, Logan has an altercation with an old man in the library. The man sprinkles magic dust on Logan's face and, as a result, Logan discovers that he can speak only in puns:

   > Benedict groaned, then said: "Hey, let's try the hardware store. They have tons of stuff."
   > "Great. Let's lumber over there and see if we can nail down a couple oxymorons," I said.

* *Gimme Cracked Corn and I Will Share* by Kevin O'Malley. The puns in this zany picture book are simple enough that primary writers will enjoy them.

* *Private I. Guana: The Case of the Missing Chameleon* by Nina Laden: "I stopped first to check in with Officer Croaker, the bullfrog chief of police, who had a habit of jumping to conclusions . . ."

* *The Phantom Tollbooth* by Norton Juster. This novel is chock-full of puns and language play: "I'm the Whether Man, not the Weather Man, for after all it's more important to know whether there will be weather than what the weather will be."

* *Pun and Games: Jokes, Riddles, Daffynitions, Tairy Fales, Rhymes, and More Word Play for Kids* by Richard Lederer. The book clearly explains various kinds of puns in a way that students will be able to grasp. In addition, this book invites kids to try their hands at pun-creation:

   > Here are ten real signs. Supply the missing words.
   > On a diaper service. Rock a _____ baby.

Sharing examples like these will pique your students' curiosity. While you read them aloud it will be tempting to stop and explain how a particular pun works. You want students to be in on the joke but, at the same time, I would caution against overexplaining. Rather, I suggest we get in the habit of leaving a space—a pause or silence—after we read a pun, so students have time for the multiple meanings to sink in.

Expecting students to instantly start using puns in their own writing is akin to planting asparagus, which must grow for two years before it produces an edible stalk. Don't be surprised if students take a long time before they take the risk and actually try this in their own writing. And when they do, the puns they concoct may turn out to be clumsy, obvious, or confusing. It's important for us to be patient. We should value their attempts first, and their results second.

But I'd hate to end this chapter on a serious note. After all, the word *pun* rhymes with *fun*. If we want our kids to enjoy experimenting with puns, we ought to do so, as well. Hey, did you hear the one about the guy who sent ten different puns to ten friends, with the hope that at least one of the puns would make them laugh? Unfortunately, no pun in ten did.

Idioms / Expressions

**If you don't stop whining
I'm going to cloud up and rain all over you!**

Father to child in supermarket

I was visiting an old college friend one time when one of his neighbors came by to chat. During our conversation this woman commented on my friend's fifteen-year-old daughter, who had recently blossomed into a striking young woman.

"She has legs up to her eyebrows," the woman remarked.

The image created by this expression made me burst out laughing; it was the perfect way to describe the leggy teen.

(Note: while there may be technical distinctions between idioms and expressions, I use the terms interchangeably in this chapter.)

A sentence should be clear, concise, and straightforward. Or should it be? In addition to a slew of precise nouns and verbs, our language includes a rich smorgasbord of idioms and colloquialisms that allow any writer to express a range of ideas. An idiom is a phrase whose meaning cannot be determined by the literal definition of the phrase itself, but refers instead to a figurative meaning known only through common use. Our language is filled with too many to count:

Let's try to *get on the same page* with him.

You're *grasping at straws*.

I *dodged a bullet* when Michael *picked up the check*.

He had a pimple *smack dab* in the middle of his forehead.

Obama won a string of primaries, but Hillary Clinton had *one more trick up her sleeve*. The hope of seating the Florida and Michigan delegations was her *ace in the hole*.

Expressions must be understood as a word group, a team of words that work together to communicate an idea or a concept. When we say: "Don't beat around the bush—please cut to the chase," a faithful word-by-word translation of these idioms won't accurately convey what they mean. For this reason, students with limited English will need additional help in assimilating English idioms. But it's not merely ELLs who will struggle with idioms. Kids are notoriously concrete in their thinking so don't be surprised if an expression such as "You hit the nail on the head" throws them for a loop.

The idioms and expressions that populate our language have come from a wide variety of sources:

Myths and fables: *Achilles heel* and *sour grapes*
War: *shell-shocked* and *bite the bullet*
Theater: *break a leg* and *bring down the house*
Sports: *two strikes against you* and *down to the wire*
Business: *the 800-pound gorilla* and *downsize*
Aeronautics: *pushing the envelope* and *Houston, we have a problem*
Religion: *turn the other cheek* and *an eye for an eye, a tooth for a tooth*

Once again, it was Shakespeare who gave rise to many popular expressions still in use today:

A laughingstock (*The Merry Wives of Windsor*)
A sorry sight (*Macbeth*)
As dead as a doornail (*Henry VI*)
Eaten out of house and home (*Henry IV*, Part 2)
Fair play (*The Tempest*)
I will wear my heart upon my sleeve (*Othello*)
In a pickle (*The Tempest*)
In stitches (*Twelfth Night*)
In the twinkling of an eye (*The Merchant of Venice*)
Mum's the word (*Henry VI*, Part 2)
Neither here nor there (*Othello*)
Send him packing (*Henry IV*)
Set your teeth on edge (*Henry IV*)

There's method in my madness (*Hamlet*)
Too much of a good thing (*As You Like It*)
Vanish into thin air (*Othello*)

Many colloquial expressions have geographical roots. When we moved from New Hampshire to Alabama we encountered many unfamiliar expressions. One day I went to register our kids for school but had forgotten to bring in their medical records. I asked one of the teachers if I could bring the forms to school the next morning.

"You might could," the woman replied, rubbing her chin. "You might could."

I have a weakness for expressions, especially new ones I've never before heard.

Cool as the underside of a pillow
Let's run it up the flagpole and see who salutes
Yard sale (when a skier spectacularly wipes out, sending his skis and gear in all different directions)

It has been said that poetry is what gets lost in the translation, but the same holds true for expressions. Because they are rooted in one language or culture, most expressions don't translate very well.

Setsuko Tsugihara, a former schoolteacher in Japan, has translated several of my children's books into Japanese. We developed a system whereby she would e-mail questions whenever she needed clarification about what I meant to say. The process was eye-opening. I quickly discovered that while most English words (*house, brother, doctor*) have a corollary in Japanese, many English idioms often do not. Here are a few excerpts from our e-mail correspondence. The first three exchanges took place while she was translating my memoir *Marshfield Dreams: When I Was a Kid* (2005a).

*I loved baseball almost as much as War. I played **pick up games** all over the neighborhood. Even when my friends weren't around, there were always enough kids in my family to form two teams.*
Setsuko: What is pick up games? Isn't it baseball games?

*"And there's a snug henhouse for cold nights," Mr. Waters said. "Believe me, your roosters **got it made in the shade**."*
Setsuko: Does *it* mean *henhouse*? Could you rewrite easier way?

*By Christmas vacation, Mom was going around saying, "**I'm a house**, aren't I?"*
Nobody disagreed. She looked like she was about to burst.
Setsuko: Does this mean her belly is a house for a baby?

The most hilarious exchanges occurred when Setsuko was trying to translate one particular expression from *Fig Pudding* (1996).

*"All right, everybody **wake up and die right**!" Grandma said.*
Setsuko: Is this a sort of old saying? Can I translate it literally?
I answered: This is just an old saying my grandmother used to say. It means "Act lively! Wake up!" Maybe you have a similar saying in Japanese.

I thought this issue was resolved but a few days later Setsuko e-mailed again: "Can I ask a little bit more about *wake up and die right*? According to your e-mail, I think the original meaning is as follows: If you wake up early and move your body enough, you can live a long life and have the fortune. Am I almost right? There's a similar old saying in Japanese: The early bird catches the worm."

I replied, "Well, you are almost right but you are being too literal. *Wake up and die right* is an old-fashioned expression that means: Get lively! Let's get going! We say, Shake a leg! The translation should say something to this effect. We also have the saying for the early bird catches the worm, but that's not exactly right here."

Expressions and Humor

Many expressions are metaphorical by implying a comparison between two things: "They are wrong to drag her through the mud" or "He's not the sharpest knife in the drawer." It's interesting to note that a well-known expression can be distorted or reversed to create a pun:

Demons are a ghoul's best friend.

This sentence contains two puns: *demon/diamond* and *ghoul/girl*. But you don't really get the joke unless you are familiar with the old expression: "Diamonds are a girl's best friend."

> *I used to be a lumberjack, but I couldn't hack it, so they gave me the ax.*

A rare double pun! But this joke, too, falls flat unless the listener is acquainted with the underlying expressions "couldn't hack it" and "gave me the ax." The joke fizzles if the listener takes these words literally. This suggests that when kids delve into jokes that rely on language play, there's more going on than we might imagine.

"The recipient of a joke needs to be able to recognize the instance of broken (or merely bent) linguistic rules," writes Delia Chiaro in her book *The Language of Jokes: Analysing Verbal Play*. "In other words his/her linguistic knowledge requires a high standard of proficiency to be able to deal with the ambiguities and hidden traps of . . . the English language" (1992, 13).

Expressions and Their Origins

The origins of many expressions have been obscured over time.

> I thought Ellen Page was great in *Juno*, but my brother insists she's just another *flash in the pan*.

You might guess that this expression harks back to the California gold rush in the 1800s. Prospectors who panned for gold became excited when they saw something glint in the pan, only to have their hopes dashed when it proved not to be gold but a mere "flash in the pan."

In fact, the expression goes much further back, to the 1600s. Flintlock muskets had a small pan to ignite the gunpowder, which would then fire the bullet. But often these guns would fail to fire properly. When the gunpowder flared up without a bullet being fired, it was known as a "flash in the pan."

One way to bring students into the world of expressions might be to invite them to investigate the origins of various expressions:

Salt it away
Mind your Ps and Qs
Dead ringer
Don't throw the baby out with the bathwater
Don't beat a dead horse
Bite the bullet
Scuttlebutt
Crack a smile
Wouldn't know him from Adam

Clichés

Clichés are the wilted flowers in the garden of idioms and expressions. Once upon a time they must have sounded fresh and meaningful, but they became so overexposed they now drag down a sentence more than enhance it. Even popular new expressions—"My bad" or "Let's not go there"—quickly become clichés if they are used too often. The list of common clichés is long and growing:

Lock, stock, and barrel
The big cheese
Off his rocker
In the nick of time
At the drop of a hat
Cry over spilled milk *or* cry wolf
Taken to the cleaners
Selling like hotcakes
Don't judge a book by its cover
Take the bull by its horns
Busy as a bee

The subject of clichés could provoke some lively discussion in the classroom because the line between an expression and a cliché is not absolute. While some clichés are fairly obvious—*pretty as a picture*—others might not be so clear-cut—*in the home stretch*. While researching clichés I uncovered these:

Garden of Weedin
I need your help like a kangaroo needs a purse
Fell out of the ugly tree and hit every branch on the way down

These three expressions may technically be considered clichés, but I confess they were new to me, and made me chuckle.

Certainly clichés are to be avoided, but they are not lethal. Skilled writers of every age can resuscitate a limp cliché by altering it in some way. Todd, a fourth grader, wrote a story with this charming sentence:

I thought it was raining cats and dogs but when I went outside it was only raining *kittens* and *puppies*.

Inventing Expressions

Some expressions are lighthearted; others plumb deeper waters. For my money, the best ones are home-baked and personal.

"Once my son, Jamie, begged and begged for a new bicycle," remembers Cyrene Wells, a writer and teacher in Machiasport, Maine. "We took him to the L.L. Bean Outlet, bought him a new, fairly expensive bike. On the way out of the store he asked, in front of cousins and aunts and uncles, if he could have a new water bottle, too. Today 'sounds like a water bottle' is a phrase we use in our family to suggest that someone is asking for a bit much."

I'll never forget the time my best friend from college, Jim Vojcsik (pronounced Voy-Check), came to visit my wife and me. The first night we had a lively dinner conversation. After we cleared the dishes Jim went upstairs to use the bathroom. I fully expected that we would continue our discussion, or perhaps play cards and listen to music. I waited and waited for him to reappear, but he did not. When I went upstairs I was stunned to see that his bedroom door was closed—he had gone to bed.

That incident happened at least fifteen years ago. But even today if either my wife or I sneak off to bed early, we refer to it as "pulling a Vojcsik."

I think it's important to give students permission to alter common expressions or, even better, to create their own. Young writers who do so demonstrate a high level of confidence and control. Tania, a seventh grader, wrote a poignant poem in which she alters a familiar word. It is a simple poem but the language play makes it memorable.

> *My friend is no longer here.*
> *No more playing at the park.*
> *Only a hug and a goodbye.*
>
> *But is it a goodbye*
> *or a bad-bye?*
>
> *I wonder if I'll ever see her again.*
> *There are no goodbyes,*
> *only bad-byes.*

Bringing It to the Writing Workshop

In Chapter 16, you'll find two craft lessons about idioms and expressions that will help students become aware of these powerful tools for writing.

Craft Lessons: Expressions

Related Children's Books

*   *And The Dish Ran Away with the Spoon* by Janet Stevens and Susan Stevens Crummel. This picture book is crammed with expressions that are used in a playful or humorous way.
*   *Roberto the Insect Architect* by Nina Laden.
*   *Stink and the Incredible Super-Galactic Jawbreaker* by Megan McDonald. This book, as well as the others in the terrific Stink series, includes a great deal of discussion of idioms and expressions. Highly recommended.
*   *Attack of the Valley Girls* by Greg Trine. There's a lot of great language play in this book, as well as in the others in the Melvin Beederman, Superhero series, including fun with well-known expressions.

Idioms and expressions allow writers to convey abstract ideas that are otherwise hard to put into words. If we regularly share them with our students, they will become more aware and may start collecting (or creating) their own. Expressions may not necessarily be the shortest distance between two points but, pound for pound, they include some of the most potent power tools any writer could have.

Allusions

**You've got as much chance of seeing that money
as seeing Custer ride back from Little Bighorn.**

Eric A. Kimmel, *Four Dollars and Fifty Cents*

An allusion is an implied or direct reference to almost anything: a person, place, myth, movie, or historical event. When a new homeowner walks into his house and announces—"That's one small step for man, one giant leap for my debt"—we recognize the ironic reference to Neil Armstrong's immortal words.

Is it overly ambitious to expect elementary students to use allusion in their writing? No. Making allusions is something people do quite naturally, even young people. When my son Robert was two years old, he loved books, and often found clever ways to refer to them during everyday talk. We had a collection of nursery rhymes and traditional poems that was among his favorites. One morning, while he was in his high chair, I asked if he was done eating breakfast. With a sly smile he declared: "Yes sir, yes sir, three bags full!"

Another morning, apropos of nothing, Robert suddenly declared: "Genevieve, noblest dog in France, you shall have your vengeance!" I recognized this line from *Madeline* by Ludwig Bemelmans, which was one of his favorite books.

When Robert was seven, he took the last chocolate chip cookie off the plate. This enraged his little brother, Joseph.

"You are so *stupid*, Robert! That was mine!"

"Now simmer down my pot of clay . . . ," Robert said.

I immediately recognized this line, too; he had borrowed it from *Strega Nona* (dePaola 1975). Many adults have similar stories they could share about their children.

An allusion serves an important function in writing by allowing the reader to understand a concept by relating it to a familiar story or character in that story:

My father is no Scrooge, but with his salary as a security guard he can't afford to take us to a fancy restaurant.

Although some allusions are direct and explicit ("His family welcomed him home like the Prodigal son"), writers frequently do not explain their allusions. By not explaining an allusion you create a space, making room for the reader to become cocreator. You can accomplish this by using an indirect allusion. If I'm writing about the fall of Eliot Spitzer, disgraced ex-governor of New York, I might say, "Spitzer was a rising star, a man some believed would one day become president. But he flew too close to the sun . . ."

This, of course, would be an indirect allusion to the Daedalus and Icarus myth. To include such an allusion I must trust that the reader and I have a shared cultural experience. I'm assuming/hoping that the reader knows the basic details of this myth: that Daedalus fashioned wings made from feathers and wax for his son, Icarus, but that the wax melted when Icarus flew too close to the sun, causing his death. The allusion provides a striking way to suggest that acting recklessly can lead to one's demise.

On the other hand, I might have used a different allusion, perhaps to Homer's *Odyssey*—"Unfortunately, Spitzer heard the Sirens' haunting song, and couldn't get it out of his head"—which would allow me to shade the meaning differently.

Allusions can be a potent and persuasive kind of descriptive tool. They can be very useful to a writer because of the way they encapsulate complex ideas, events, or emotions in a quick powerful image:

When the iceberg struck Enron, the big ship started taking on water, but there weren't nearly enough lifeboats for all the people who needed them.

I have a friend who has had terrible luck in her relationships with men. She once remarked that she might write a screenplay about her dismal love life.

"I'm going to call it *Night of the Living Dorks*," she added dryly.

I laughed. And it struck me that an allusion is similar to a pun in that it allows the mind to occupy two spaces—a dismal dating life and the classic horror film—at the same time.

Writers down through the ages—playwrights, poets, essayists, novelists—have made generous use of allusions in their work. Although he wasn't a religious man, Hemingway used many biblical allusions in *The Old Man and the Sea*. In that novel he describes Santiago supporting the fishing line in ways that suggest Jesus carrying the cross. And at one point Hemingway portrays the old man as crying "Ay" and goes on to say that "there is no translation for this word and perhaps it is just a noise such as a man might make, involuntarily, feeling the nail go through his hands and into the wood" (1981, 107).

Authors of children's books have also found allusion to be a useful tool. In *Piggie Pie!* (1995), a marvelous picture book by Margie Palatini, Gritch the Witch visits a farm in search of eight plump piggies. The book includes allusions to popular stories, including "Old MacDonald" and *The Wizard of Oz*. (L. Frank Baum's novel itself contained many allusions. For instance, the yellow brick road is an allusion to the gold currency standard, a subject of hot debate at the time. And the city of Oz is an allusion to Washington, DC, where nothing much ever gets done.)

Andrew Clements's novel *Frindle* involves a pitched battle between a third-grade student named Nicholas and his teacher Mrs. Granger. At one point the teacher is referred to as "The Lone Granger," an allusion to a TV show that most children today probably don't even know.

When I began looking for allusions I was struck by how many journalists and contemporary experts use them. For example, when Warren Buffett was asked to explain the dismal performance of his Berkshire Hathaway company in 2002, the genial billionaire replied: "I violated the Noah rule: predicting rain doesn't count; building arks does."

In 2008 the *Boston Globe* ran a sports story about Boston College's upset of the University of North Carolina basketball team, which had been ranked number one in the country. Julian Benbow, sportswriter, used a film allusion to describe the way Boston College's Tyrese Rice wanted to control the tempo of the basketball game.

The way Sandra Bullock eyed the needle on the speedometer of the racing bus in Speed*, Rice had to control the pace, knowing that if it got too fast the Tar Heels' offense would ignite. (2008)*

When it comes to sportswriters, most would rank the *Boston Globe*'s Dan Shaughnessy as one of the very best in the game. In addition to his regular columns,

Shaughnessy has also written several best-selling sports books, including *The Curse of the Bambino* (2004). Shaughnessy often includes allusions in his columns. Here's an excerpt from a column he wrote about the rivalry between the Red Sox and the New York Yankees:

> *There are 30 games to play and the Sox lead the Yankees by seven after last night's 5-3 loss to the Bronx Bombers. It's a bizarro season. The Sox are the secure team. It is the once-dominant Yanks who are scrambling, scuffling for a wild card, spitting up pieces of their broken luck. (2007)*

Here we see Shaughnessy inventing a new word—*bizarro*—or at least a new variation of a word. The vivid image in the last seven words—"spitting up pieces of their broken luck"—is borrowed without attribution from the lyrics to "Aqualung," a song by Jethro Tull.

In another column, Shaughnessy described Los Angeles Lakers coach Phil Jackson after his team lost the final game of the NBA Championships to the Boston Celtics: "The Celtics ran to a 79–48 lead midway through the third while the poet on the Laker bench just stood back and let it all be" (2008).

The last eight words are an allusion to a line from the song "Jungleland" by Bruce Springsteen. When I interviewed Dan Shaughnessy, I asked him about his penchant for inserting such allusions in his columns.

DS: *Not all journalists are interested in the craft part of writing, but I am. I do things like that to make the piece interesting for the reader, but I also do it for my own fun.*

RF: That reference to "Jungleland" is pretty obscure. Does it bother you that most of your readers probably won't pick up on it?

DS: *Not at all. If I use it, and maybe only one person in twenty gets it, that's good enough for me.*

RF: What considerations do you have when you think about including language play in your columns? Do you ever worry about putting too much in, or going too far?

DS: *If it is going to stop the reader, or get in the way of the flow of the writing, you probably shouldn't do it.*

RF: During this interview you referred to language play as craft. But it's a very playful kind of craft.

DS: *Sure it's playful. We're writing sports here. We ought to be able to have some fun, right?*

Most of Shaughnessy's allusions come from pop culture, which brings up an important issue. While student writers will often allude directly or indirectly to popular movies, TV shows, and video games, teachers may discourage young writers from making reference to popular media. I suggest we reconsider this stance.

In "Popular Culture as a Literacy Tool," an essay in Tom Newkirk's recent book (2009), the author puts forth an eloquent argument that adopting a more generous view toward popular story types (Star Wars, Spider-Man, SpongeBob SquarePants, etc.) will go a long way toward keeping children (especially boys) engaged in reading and writing. And he challenges those who would look down on popular culture and dismiss it as inferior fluff: "To assert that some genres are, by their very nature, 'authentic' and others are 'inauthentic,' is at its root, simply disguised censorship. It is an arbitrary assertion of literary preference" (2009, 105).

Indeed, popular culture offers many ways of helping students get a feel for allusion. Middle or secondary students readily relate to the TV series *The Simpsons*. Nearly every episode includes a direct or indirect allusion to a song, movie, famous personality, or historical event.

*   In one episode the mayor says, "Ich bin ein Springfielder," a reference to JFK's famous speech.
*   When Sideshow Bob is in jail, his prison number is 24601, which is the same number as Jean Valjean's in *Les Misérables*.
*   The morning after chopping off the head of the Jebediah Springfield statue in "The Telltale Head," Bart wakes up with the head beside him in his bed, an allusion to the famous horse's head scene in *The Godfather*.

Many of the allusions in *The Simpsons* are subtle; it's a pretty good bet that most kids won't get them.

"Everybody doesn't have to get every joke," says Matt Groening, the creator of *The Simpsons*. "People really appreciate not being condescended to. . . . I love the idea that we put in jokes the kids don't get. And later, when they grow up and read a few books and go to college and watch the show again, they can get it on a completely different level" (Davis 1999).

Bringing It to the Writing Workshop

An allusion is a dramatic writing tool. It provides a way to remind the reader of people and events from other books and invites the reader to see the current scene or situation in the light of this additional information.

Craft Lesson: Allusions

When Writers Refer to Something Outside the Story (K–2), page 110
Using Allusion in Your Writing (5+), page 126

Related Children's Books

*   *Each Peach Pear Plum* by Janet and Allan Ahlberg. For very young readers.
*   *Piggie Pie!* by Margie Palatini. Highly recommended.
*   *The Butter Battle Book* by Dr. Seuss. A clear allusion to the Cold War. Also *The Lorax.*
*   Melvin Beederman, Superhero series by Greg Trine. This zany series contains many implicit allusions to other superhero stories, including Batman:

    > *Suddenly one of the pretzels started ringing.*
    > *Melvin jumped. "Holy high-tech snack food, I forgot all about my pretzel phone" (2007).*

*   A Series of Unfortunate Events (Books 1–13) by Lemony Snicket. Characters in this series include Mr. Poe (who has two sons named Edgar and Allan), Coach Genghis, and Vice Principal Nero, who makes students sit through six-hour concerts (an allusion to Emperor Nero, who fiddled while Rome burned).
*   *The Willoughbys* by Lois Lowry. This comical spoof is crammed with allusions and is perfect for the sensibilities of upper-middle-grade readers.

* *Summer Reading Is Killing Me!* by Jon Scieszka. This adventure in the Time Warp Trio series is supersaturated with humorous allusions to other books: "We stepped over a very hungry caterpillar eating his way through a dictionary. . . . We made our way through a crowd made up of Robinson Crusoe, a blue moose, Julie with some wolves, a snowman, a plain and tall lady named Sarah, a kid with a hatchet, and a very confused-looking Robin Hood helping Eeyore reattach his tail."

10

Harnessing the Supple Power of Sentences

The pouches under his eyes were like purses that contained the smuggled memories from a disappointing life.

Graham Greene, *A Burnt-Out Case*

In the United States the mass production of goods began around 1910. That's when factories were built with automated assembly lines capable of churning out Model T cars exactly the same, one after another.

Writers, too, are involved in the business of mass production. We produce large quantities of words. I recently saw a writer on a TV talk show who bragged that he had "a million words in print." Unlike mass production, however, uniformity is *not* the goal writers have when it comes to creating sentences. In fact, writing the same kind of sentences over and over is something writers try hard to avoid.

Skilled writers put forth a variety of sentences, but variety per se is not the goal either. Rather, writers craft custom-made sentences, each one designed for a particular purpose. Let's see how they do it, and how we might expand student repertoires in terms of the kinds of sentences they might write.

Breaking the Rules

There's a famous story in my family about an event that took place at the town pool in Paramus, New Jersey, when our oldest son, Taylor, was five. JoAnn was sitting with Taylor in an enclosed area with a wading pool, a space reserved for small children and their parents. At one point JoAnn left the fenced-in area to fetch some suntan lotion. She could still watch Taylor through the chain-link fence, but when Taylor realized that she was no longer with him he got upset. Angrily he pointed to a sign that stated: "Parents Must Stay with Children in This Area."

"You're breaking the rules!" Taylor cried to JoAnn. "You're breaking the rules!"

JoAnn, who didn't realize that Taylor had even seen that sign, assured Taylor that it was okay because she could still keep an eye on him. But he wasn't satisfied until JoAnn returned to the designated area.

This story reveals a side of Taylor's character. Like many oldest children (including me), he had a penchant for following the rules, and never failed to notice it when stated rules were not being followed.

Many young writers are rule-bound, too. Teachers have reinforced the conventions of grammatically correct sentences—begin with a capital, include a subject and a verb, end with a period—and that's not all bad. But if we are not careful, this focus on convention and correctness can lead to writing that is lifeless and monotonous. Often when I read student writing I find myself hungering for a different kind of sentence, something striking and new, even if it violates the rules we might find in a grammar book.

The evidence would indicate that many professional writers do not feel bound by rules of sentences. Dip into a picture book like *The Great Fuzz Frenzy* (Stevens and Crummel) and you'll find sentence fragments galore. Here's a section from *Gorky Rises* by William Steig (1986): "Very carefully, he put in a bit of his father's clear cognac. Better. But something still was missing. What?"

Often a writer will deliberately use a run-on sentence. A well-known example can be found near the end of Maurice Sendak's book *Where the Wild Things Are*: "The wild things roared their terrible roars and gnashed their terrible teeth and rolled their terrible eyes and showed their terrible claws but Max stepped into his private boat and waved good-bye . . ." (1988).

A long sentence like this creates a headlong rush of momentum. It works like a fast-forward button on a DVD player, shoving the story forward. It would be interesting to ask students to find other examples where authors break a particular sentence rule, and to consider why they have decided to do so. It is hardly ever a random endeavor. When authors break a rule, they almost always have a reason for doing so.

Short, Snappy Sentences

Readers will be numbed if forced to read too many sentences of the same length, structure, and cadence. One way of avoiding this is to vary the pacing of sentences by inserting brief phrases. I recently read the first two books in the Lunch Lady series by Jarrett Krosoczka. While reading these graphic novels, I was struck by how often the characters spoke in bursts of one, two, or three words. This keeps the energy high and surely contributes to the "readability" of such texts.

A short burst of words is a great way to convey speed and urgency. Louise Borden does this effectively in her powerful picture book *The Little Ships: The Heroic Rescue at Dunkirk in World War II.*

> *Hurry . . . Not much time! . . .*
> *Too many men . . . Not enough ships!*

One principle I follow is that the length and cadence of the sentences should reflect what's happening in the story. When things are hunky-dory, the accompanying sentences can also be smooth and flowing. But at a point in the story where there is a sudden eruption of action, or when events spin out of control, short, choppy sentences are a good way to reflect this.

Controlling the Tempo in a Series of Sentences

No sentence exists in isolation; a writer must also consider how it rubs up against the other sentences on either side. A series of sentences can work together to create a particular effect, such as when several sentences begin in the same way. On the first page of William Steig's picture book *Amos & Boris*, we find three sentences about Amos the mouse, the main character: "He loved the ocean. He loved the smell of sea air. He loved to hear the surf sounds." The repetition of "He loved" links these sentences together, creates a satisfying rhythm, and establishes Amos's character.

This is another example of how important it is to write with the ear, in this case focusing on the sound and rhythm in a series of sentences. A writer may similarly decide to construct a string of sentences such that they build upon themselves:

He skinned his knees playing soccer. He had gotten banged into the boards while playing hockey. But nothing in those two sports had prepared him for the unrelenting violence of lacrosse.

This is known as the 1-2-3 cadence. I was made aware of this idea by Dan Feigelson, friend and author of *Practical Punctuation* (2008). I don't think it is coincidental that Dan, who is a musician, would be alive to cadence and rhythm. Notice that the first sentence is the shortest, the second a bit longer, and the third the longest of all. You can drum out the cadence—ba bum, ba da bum, ba da da da da da *BUM*—and hear how the first two sentences set up the power of the third. This can also be done in reverse, the 3-2-1 cadence, where two longer sentences get the reader ready for a short, powerful one.

Plenty of times I had eyeballed a dead squirrel or raccoon on the roads around town. I had viewed dead goldfish, hamsters, and hermit crab. But never a dead person.

Sentence Reversals

For forty years Jackson Browne has been one of our most skilled lyricists. In Browne's most recent CD, *Time the Conqueror*, a line in the first song caught my ear: "In my mind I'm certain—nothing's certain yet."

Here he starts a sentence going one way and then flips it around to go in the opposite direction. This creates tension, and adds energy to what could have been a humdrum sentence.

This is known as a sentence reversal—a rhetorical flourish can be dazzling when done skillfully and has been used by many authors.

"You have to be out of the sea really to know how good it is to be in it," he thought. (Steig)

"I meant what I said
And I said what I meant . . .
An elephant's faithful
One hundred per cent!" (Seuss)

Calvin Trillin named this pyrotechnic a "reversible raincoat sentence," a term that political speechwriters quickly seized upon. President John F. Kennedy is one of many politicians who saw the power of such reversals, and frequently used them in his speeches: "Ask not what your country can do for you—ask what you can do for your country."

No doubt the sentence reversal will be a stretch for many students, but some will be intrigued to play with this strategy. A list of examples can be found in Appendix D.

Bringing It to the Writing Workshop

When it comes to creating a fresh kind of sentence, the possibilities truly are endless. A writer can create a sentence that is unusually short (or long); a declarative sentence where the subject is implied: "Stop!"; or a sentence with an interjection embedded in it: "When I found a wallet containing five twenty dollar bills, I tucked it in my pocket—Be honest: wouldn't you?—and hurried back home."

In Chapter 16 you'll find six craft lessons designed to encourage student writers to experiment with sentences and expand what they are already doing.

Craft Lessons: The Power of Sentences

If DNA molecules are the building blocks of life, sentences are the building blocks of writing. We should do whatever we can to help our young writers get comfortable with sentences in all their forms.

* Encourage students to be on the lookout for sentences that are interesting, odd, or unusual, or for ones that break the standard grammar rules.
* Ask students to consider not just what the author is doing but why.
* Don't encourage formulaic writing.
* Give kids plenty of freedom to try to invent new kinds of sentences of their own.
* The children's books listed in the bibliography contain a rich source of striking sentences. Search the bibliography to locate books that are available to you and read them to find examples for your mini-lessons and models for your students.

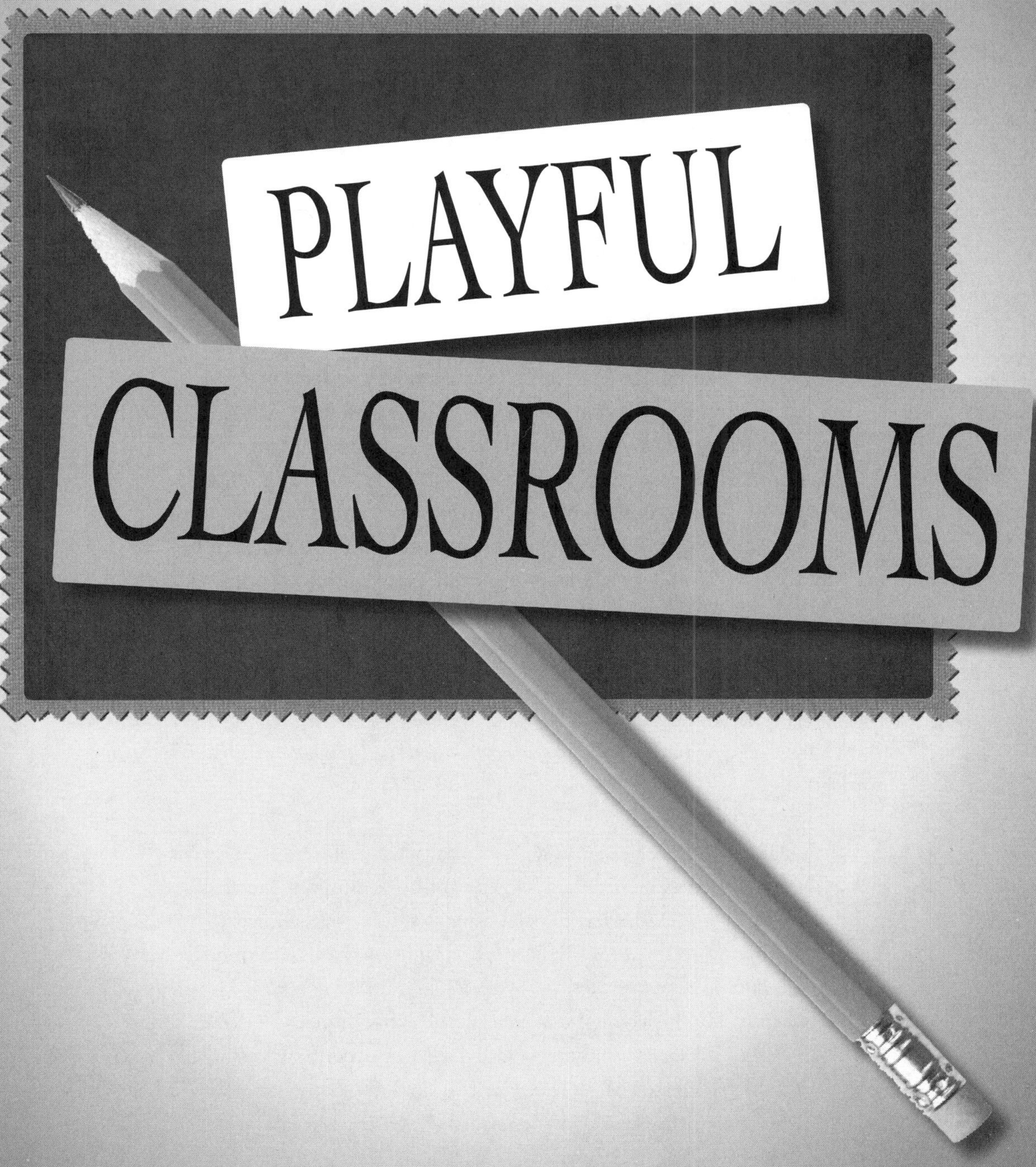
PLAYFUL
CLASSROOMS

11

Reclaiming the Play in Language Play

**Stay alive, refreshed in language! Listen to little toddlers
bopping metaphors around the room like balloons.
Let language zip and lean, sound can lead you,
be surprised as you are writing. I play with words
every day and I am going to play right now. It takes me
where I need to go, into the real content, and into the
serious hard places, too. Experimenting means**
anything goes. **We need to keep doing that on our pages
if they are to keep glittering and waking us up.**

Naomi Shihab Nye

As we saw in Chapter 5, educators have long valued play as an ideal environment for learning.

* Piaget considered play an activity that gave children a way to develop and refine concepts before they had the ability to think in the abstract.
* Vygotsky emphasized the social aspects of play. He argued that during play children were able to think in more complex ways than in their everyday lives, and could make up rules, use symbols, and create narratives. He believed that when a child is playing he is "a head taller than himself" (1978, 102).
* Mihaly Csikszentmihalyi developed the notion of flow: a state of deep focus in which a person is so immersed in an activity that they lose all sense of time. Flow brings an intrinsic reward which tends to make an activity some-

thing a person wishes to engage in for its own sake. In his view, the flow zone is an uber-rich learning environment. Csikszentmihalyi believed that games and other forms of play create ideal conditions for flow.

Many educators, then, have celebrated play as an ideal environment for learning. Parents willingly steep their children in it. But the word *play* sounds suspiciously laid-back and nonrigorous in today's test-centric educational world. Where does it fit in today's writing classroom?

Parameters of Play

Imagine three friends come over to play with your nine-year-old son or daughter. But first you take them aside to make a few suggestions as to how they might take advantage of this play opportunity.

"There are some old boards stacked next to the garage," you begin. "Maybe you could play with them by building a teepee or a yurt, like the Native Americans made. Oh, and you know that pile of gravel at the edge of the yard? You could play by sorting the rocks into categories: igneous, metamorphic, or sedimentary. If you finish with that, why don't you arrange the stones on the driveway in the pattern of star constellations?"

My kids would fire lasers at me should I ever attempt such a stunt. Real play, of course, looks nothing like this. In the first place, there's no choice. The play is being orchestrated by an adult. This "play" looks suspiciously like homework in disguise. It's reminiscent of the famous scene in *The Adventures of Tom Sawyer* (1994) in which Tom Sawyer convinces his friends that whitewashing a fence is actually fun (play) instead of work. But as every reader knows, Tom is pulling a fast one. Let's not confuse *play* with *task* when we invite young writers to play with language. It seems dishonest to assign students a task while pretending that it is play.

From the playground to the classroom, play is on the decline. You can feel it the moment you step into schools. It's rare to enter a school and hear children singing with their teacher. Recess minutes have been severely pruned. There's a paucity of play in kindergartens, which have become much more academic than they were ten years ago. Teachers feel a continuous, grinding pressure to boost test scores. The current educational climate inspired the following poem from my book *A Writing Kind of Day* (2005b):

Bad Weather

They're predicting a big term paper
due to arrive on Monday morning.

Tuesday the forecast looks bad:
intense DOL and grammar drills.

Wednesday will be a scorcher
when the state writing test arrives.

Thursday there's a high probability
of five-paragraph essays.

Friday should bring some relief
when scattered poetry blows in.

What then do we mean by play? What are some of its essential elements? I suggest that play is:

* ***Joyful and enjoyable.*** Jane Yolen described to me a recent visit to see her grandchildren, five-year-old twin girls.
  "The girls and I played a word game about words that are spelled the same way backwards and forwards," she said. "We found *mom, pop, dad, tot.* And when they came home from school, they not only had remembered all the words we thought of, but Caroline had figured out several more: *bob* (a boy they knew), *bib*, and *pep*. Not to be outdone, Amelia came up with another herself: *wow*! Then I showed them an entire sentence that was a palindrome: *Madam I'm Adam.* Since they have an Uncle Adam, we had a huge giggle about that. And best of all, it was *fun*!"

Ease, relaxation, pleasure, and fun are essential elements of play. Fun brings with it a healthy dollop of humor. Expect laughter. If you want to promote play as a means of language learning, fun is not just a nice concept to shoot for, it's essential. The math is fairly basic: No fun = no play = diminished learning.

* *Social—not isolated.* It is true that people enjoy working on crossword puzzles and other kinds of solitary language play, but Jane Yolen's story reminds us how much human beings enjoy playing together.

* *Hands-on/experiential.* When our youngest son became semiaddicted to Guitar Hero, my wife took the plunge and tried it for herself. This won his stubborn admiration. Play is the ultimate constructivist activity—it's about doing rather than observing. As teachers, we must be willing to peel off our socks and wade into the water alongside our students.

* *Supersaturated with talk.* Talk plays a starring role when it comes to learning in general and play in particular. Children who are playing often engage in a loud, ragged chatter, a rapid-paced conversation that doesn't follow any preset guidelines or role sheets. Talk is a comfortable medium for helping students make connections and assimilate new concepts.

* *Experimental.* Hey, let's see what would happen if we changed this around and tried this . . .

* *Open-ended,* as opposed to a closed exercise where we give students a text and ask them to find predetermined examples of metaphor, simile, idiom, and so forth. We might bring in newspapers or magazines (or invite them to bring in their own) and let kids read through them, looking for examples of language play, striking word use, or whatever they find intriguing in this regard.

* *Reciprocal.* The information does not flow solely from the teacher down to the student. Rather, the teacher and students often find themselves learning side by side. "When did people start using the word *text* as a verb? I wonder how we could find out . . ."

* *Nonevaluative.* People engaged in language play don't fixate on mistakes. A wrong answer in a crossword puzzle is quickly erased and forgotten once the right word becomes apparent. Picture a mother going to the supermarket with her toddler son. During the drive she creates an impromptu rhyming game.

Mother: Street.
Son: *Eat!*
Mother: Ants.
Son: *Pants!*
Mother: Black.
Son: *Fack! Okay, now you do it, Mommy. Dog.*

Mother: Fog!
Son: *That's good, Mommy. Tree.*
Mother: Bee!

In such an environment a mistake (fack) is hardly worth mentioning in the exuberant verbal ping-ponging between parent and child. Such mistakes are usually the source of delight and laughter.

If you have ever played peekaboo with a toddler on an airplane, you know that even the smallest child can sustain play for an astonishing length of time. But being a grown-up is serious business; some of us have been out of the play game for too long. We may need a refresher course. I know I did.

Not long ago I played a neighborhood game of baseball with an old college buddy of mine. Jim and I divided the kids (mostly first and second graders) into two teams. I was playing shortstop. When the batter hit a ground ball to me, I moved forward to field it. But at that very moment a neighborhood dog darted in, snatched the ball before it reached my glove, and raced away. Kids from both teams dropped their gloves and started chasing the dog.

"Hey wait!" I yelled in frustration as the kids sprinted after the dog. "I've got another ball!"

But it was too late. The dog, ball, and kids had disappeared. I stood looking glumly at Jim. He gave me a rueful smile. "I think the game just changed from playing baseball to chasing the dog."

At the risk of overanalyzing this anecdote, it's worth pointing out a few things. For children, play is a fluid activity that can suddenly morph and change into something else without warning. When the neighborhood kids ran off to chase the dog in the middle of the baseball game, I was the one rigidly stuck to "staying on task" with the game at hand. For those eight-year-olds, the transition from one kind of game to another was natural and effortless.

One other thing: choice. Those neighborhood kids suddenly didn't want to play baseball anymore—they spontaneously chose a different kind of play. It's up to us to create conditions where students will want to play with language. At the same time we must be willing to revise our teaching when they choose not to do so, or opt to play in a way that is different from what we expect.

12

Igniting Pyrotechnics in the Classroom

You can only learn so much if you just follow the steps of a preset Lego design. You really learn how Legos work when you begin experimenting, testing, building something new. Kids learn language when they can manipulate and change it.

Gresham Brown, third-grade teacher

What might language play look like in the writing classroom? In this chapter we'll look at two teachers who took two different approaches.

Gresham Brown teaches third grade in Greenville, South Carolina. He wanted to try a lesson on language play with his students. Here, in Gresham's words, is what happened.

Lesson: Writing Puns

We always end our class meeting every day with two jokes, so my kids are pretty familiar with this kind of wordplay. I began the lesson by sharing poetry that showcases lots of puns. Most of the poems were taken from Douglas Florian's *Laugh-eteria.* After sharing several poems, I asked kids to describe the types of wordplay they saw, or strategies they could use. We came up with three ideas:

1. Using one word that sounds like another word:

    ketchup and *catch up*

2. Taking phrases literally—"have an open mind"

3. Using a word that has two meanings or spellings, such as *wave* or *hair*

As students went off to write, I encouraged them to try writing poems using some of these types of strategies. Here are a few of their poems:

French Fries by Ben

I went to France
and said:
Can I
have French fries?

He said how
dare you fry
our country!

No I said
I don't want your country fried
I just want some
French fries.

It Worked, But . . . by Alex

I told my Grandpa that I
had the hiccups
What should I do?
He understood.
"Hike up," he said.
"Try the Appalachian Trail."

So I went west
six months later
I came back
with
the

cold,
fever,
fleas,
but . . .
not the
hiccups.

Literally by Alaina

"Put up your hair!"
said my mother.
She gave me a hairpin.

So I unlocked the top cabinet
and put up my hair.

I REALLY
don't see why
my mother was sooooo surprised
when I came to dinner bald.

Chili by Caitlyn

I'm getting chili today.
So I brought my jacket and lunchbox.

It was
brown
brown
I mean very brown.

Can I get seconds?
I'm getting chili.

Homework by Julian

I was out of school for a few weeks
When I got back my teacher told me,
yes me
to catch up on my homework

So I did
I went to the fridge and got some ketchup
Then I got my homework,
took the Ketchup
and put it on my homework

(Julian added a sketch of our math homework covered with a ketchup blob.)

The kids really enjoyed writing today. There was an electric feel to the room. Kids were laughing and sharing with each other. Several kids were collaborating with each other, and everyone was highly engaged. I think my kids were ready for this kind of writing simply because we share so many jokes in our class. I was proud of the way they took risks and experimented with word sounds and word meanings.

Ali Marron, a fifth-grade teacher at PS 6 in Manhattan, wanted to encourage her students to experiment with language play in their writing, but wasn't sure how to proceed.

"It's such a tricky question," Ali said. "How can you nurture something the kids are unaware of? But at the same time, teaching alliteration or onomatopoeia as a lesson does risk killing the playfulness. Maybe the trick is how you teach it. I wanted to see if I could make the kids leaders of the game for a while, at least until some sizeable enthusiasm is built up."

Ali began by telling students that she was interested in wordplay, studying the various ways kids use language. That sparked an interest in the kids, who suddenly had lots of questions, such as, "What exactly is wordplay? What is a pun?"

After that, Ali kept her eyes open for examples of language play that sprouted in the class. Here are some examples of what she found.

The new fad among several girls in class is to randomly state, "Guess what? I'm half dolphin!" I guess it's from a funny scene in a show called *Sunny with a Chance* (or at least that's what I think they said). They announce, "Guess what? I'm half dolphin!" and then smile and pretend water is spraying out of their heads.

Michaela and Dominique have been friends for years and have a little ritual greeting between the two of them. I'm not sure if they made it up or got it from somewhere. It goes like this: (1) the first person says, "Achoogan" and sneezes; (2) the second person says, "Bless Yougen" and bows; (3) the first person says, "Thank yougen" and bows. I asked them where it came from, but they didn't seem to know—just one of those things that they either saw and/or it evolved naturally.

In a story by Arianne she used the phrase "un-progress report" to de-scribe the report card of a character who's failing. Later in the story (told in journal entries) the main character calls her friend "the best friend anyone could ever have" and then says, "As much as I adore her, she's not exactly the brightest bulb." Then there's a picture of a girl with a peanut for a brain.

Ellis is writing a story that begins: "Some normal words mean regular things to people. But some words mean much more to others. For me the word *mail* means a lot. It all started one summer afternoon." And then he goes on to tell the story of a piece of mail he was waiting for.

Dominique is writing a story for our realistic fiction unit called "Girl Lan-guage." It starts: "There are many languages in the world, Chinese, French, Spanish, Latin and most of all secret girl language. Yes there might be many languages, but secret girl language is the most important."

One other thing: I've discovered that my class has a secret notebook they pass around. One student borrowed the idea after reading *Please Write in This Book* [Amato] and got it started. One kid writes an entry, then hides it. The next kid that finds it (it's always hidden somewhere in the library) writes and then hides it again. It's pretty amusing, actually. All the rules are theirs. I'm totally uninvolved and had to "steal" it in order to look through it. There's the usual IM–speak all over the place: GTG, LOL, BFF, *u* for *you*. Kids boss each other around on paper ("Charlie, when you use this book, WRITE WORDS!"), make new rules, and then apologize in their next entry for being mean. Ciara starts her first letter, "Hey my peeps!" and Dominique follows with a letter beginning, "Say hay, ho, say hay, ho! Hey peeps!" Gabbie stepped it up a notch and began her letter, "Hello peoples!" When peer mediation tryouts were going on, Julia wrote, "Hey people of 5–302, it's Julia! How's it going? I'm dying to become a peer." Matthew wrote, "Hey what's up home dog it's your friend Matthew K talk to you later." It's funny, because they never speak like that in the classroom. I don't think I've ever heard one of them use the term *home dog* or call each other *peeps*. It's as if the book has become their own separate world.

Here we see two teachers approaching language play in two different ways. Gresham created a lesson on puns using playful poetry as a model. He built on his students' familiarity with poetry and with jokes. Gresham took a risk by teaching a concept he had never taught before. I think his pioneer spirit trickled down and empowered the students when they tried it in their writing.

Ali took a more organic approach. She raises an important point when she says, "I wanted to see if I could make the kids leaders of the game for a while, at least until some sizeable enthusiasm is built up." Rather than teach lessons, she made students aware of her interest in language play, and then conducted classroom research to see what her students were doing in this regard. When she looked closely, she discovered a wealth of hitherto hidden language play both in their talk and in their writing. The knowledge that Ali has gleaned could set the stage for more direct instruction in how her students could play with words in their writing.

Teachers who are interested in fostering language play need to be watchful. I'm a big fan of responsive teaching. This begins with our showing interest, observing carefully, finding examples of students using wordplay, and celebrating when it happens. Once the buzz has been created, we can teach into their curiosity and excitement.

Common Principles

Every writing teacher will approach language play in writing workshops in his or her own way; still, a few common principles emerge that are worth holding on to.

* **Use explicit language.** When we invite young writers to play with words, our message should be clear and unequivocal. Naomi Shihab Nye told

me, "I am always reminding kids to, as Kim Stafford says, 'play with their writing, not just work on it.'"

* **Prepare for surprise.** Don Murray wrote a book about writing titled *Expecting the Unexpected* (1989). This inherent paradox is ever-present in teaching as well—*planning* for kids to *spontaneously* invent something new and fresh. It's never easy to catch lightning in a bottle. But if we give students time, space, and encouragement, they will rise to the occasion.

* **Bring language play into all aspects of the writing classroom.** Chapter 16 contains specific craft lessons about language pyrotechnics. These lessons will make it easy to explore language play with students during a mini-lesson. But the mini-lesson is not the only time to talk to students about pyrotechnics. At the end of the workshop, during the share session, you might encourage other kids to pay attention to how fellow writers have played with language in their writing.

Writing conferences offer a unique one-on-one opportunity to focus on this issue. The questions we ask and comments we make can attune students to the sound of their sentences and get them in the habit of writing with the ear as well as the eye. Writing conferences give us a chance to point out and celebrate alliteration, puns, and other forms of language play. Much of this may be accidental, but when we identify it in their writing, students can claim and own what they have done.

* **Model for students.** Make a point of including puns, word jokes, and other forms of language play during your regular classroom instruction. Even better, show them examples from your own writing.

* **Tune students to language play** *outside* **the writing workshop.** You'll find many useful examples in other parts of the school day: the reading workshop, history, current events, and media. These nonwriting examples build deeper understanding in our students and set the stage for those occasions when they sit down to write.

* **Encourage talk; don't squelch it.** In both Gresham and Ali's classes, student-to-student talk (also known as "cross-talk") acted as an incubator in which students could be comfortable experimenting with words.

* **Celebrate their successes.** I have come to believe that praise is more important than we may have realized. Young writers need a great deal of affirmation and encouragement. We should make a fuss when our writers make a breakthrough in the way they use language.
* **Value the attempt; don't expect perfection.** In Gresham's third-grade class, some of the written results were better than others. Whenever students try something new, it's more important to value the attempt than to expect sterling results.

13

The Limits of Labeling: A Brief Cautionary Tale

In his mind-blowing book *The Songlines* (1988), Bruce Chatwin wrote about the Australian Aboriginal creation myths. According to Chatwin, when ancient Aboriginals spotted an animal, rock, stream, or plant, they would respond by calling out the name of that object in the form of a song. In essence, they were singing those objects into existence by naming them.

This is a haunting idea, and a reminder of how powerful naming can be. Young children quickly learn that being able to accurately name an object—"bottle" or "blankie"—goes a long way to getting their needs met. In medicine, doctors know that the first key step toward restoring someone's health involves an accurate identification of what that ailment is.

Nevertheless, we should be careful not to overstate the importance of labeling various kinds of language play: homonym, alliteration, allusion, onomatopoeia, etc. Certainly it does help to know the names of these pyrotechnics. A common language is useful in making sure that the whole class is on the same page when discussing any concept. But there is a limited amount of time in the classroom, and kids have a finite attention span for any one subject area. Given these limits, I side with usage over labeling. I'd much rather have teachers spend precious resources letting kids get a feel for language play—how it works to strengthen a sentence—than making sure they can precisely distinguish between a homophone and a homonym.

Case in point: I have recently begun work on a new picture book about the wind. I'm thinking this might become a companion text to *Twilight Comes Twice* (1997b) and *Hello, Harvest Moon* (2003). I'm doing what I always do, casting a wide net, generating ideas in my writer's notebook. Here are a few initial entries.

the wind is like a sentence
that doesn't begin with a capital
or end with a period or question mark
just one long run-on (blow-on?) sentence

Autumn wind
rattles the glass
whistles past your window
makes the branches sway
and the leaves leave

At the blustery beach
the wind plays hairdresser
parting your hair this way
and that.

All the tall grasses are whisssspering
sssssssssssss
aaaaahhhhhhhhhhh
sssssssssshhhhhhhhhhhhhh
waving in the wash of the wind.

The wind wings through the sky,
coaxing clouds to move along
like a shepherd with a pack
of fluffy sheep.

blow blow blow the dust
up through the air stream
easily breezily teasily wheezily
life is but a dream

Generating this stuff (none of which may end up in the final book) is a crucial part of my process. Notice that while these notebook ramblings are focused on the wind, at the same time they are loose, expansive, and whimsical. I'm letting my mind roam far and wide. I'm giving myself carte blanche to play and to break grammatical rules, if necessary. Anything goes, as Naomi Shihab Nye puts it.

But while I'm engrossed in this kind of language play, I'm not saying to myself, "I need more alliteration. I better weave in some fresh language, golden lines. C'mon, Ralphie boy, how about inserting a few more puns or double meanings?"

Rather, while generating these entries I'm trying to be open and receptive in an organic way to what language play possibilities might arise along the way. For instance, in the first stanza I originally wrote "run-on sentence." Then I started thinking that the wind doesn't really run but blows, which made me think of a "blow-on sentence," which felt surprising and new. While I was writing another stanza, I stumbled onto the playful confusion of *leaves* and *leave*. Later on I concocted the words *teasily* and *wheezily*.

In his book *Writing Poems*, Robert Wallace makes an important point about alliteration and assonance: "Using them is more discovering, or taking advantage of, than imposing them" (1991, 111).

Wallace's point is equally pertinent to every kind of language play mentioned in this book. *Real language play is not top down but bottoms up.* Or, to put it another way, *language play evolves from the inside out, not the outside in.*

What implication does this have for the classroom? For one thing, I don't think we should be preoccupied with teaching (and testing) the various names for these strategies. I'd rather see this time spent examining rich texts in an open-ended study of language play. It would be interesting to lead students in an author study, perhaps with a writer like William Steig, a real inquiry where students could examine the various kinds of language play that show up again and again in his books.

A similar thing might happen through deep language inquiry of a single book: *The Great Fuzz Frenzy* by Janet Stevens and Susan Stevens Crummel or, for older readers, Denise Doyen's luscious picture book *Once Upon a Twice*. After you read the book aloud, invite students to discuss (in pairs, small groups, or whole class) what they noticed in terms of language play. You might offer questions designed to promote discussion.

What sounds did you like in what we just read?
Where did the author do something you're envious of and might like to try in your own writing?

What struck you? What was surprising or unexpected about the language this author used?

Why do you think the author played with language in this way?

If we want to spark real classroom inquiry about language pyrotechnics, let's make sure that naming these techniques doesn't close down our students' thinking, but opens it up.

During a recent trip to Lubec, Maine, I spotted a bird banging on the trunk of a large pine tree not far from where I was staying. The critter really was enormous—at least a foot tall—and utterly fearless, ignoring me as I edged closer and closer. I suddenly wanted to know what kind of bird it was, so I ran inside and opened our bird book.

In the woodpecker section I found it: a pileated woodpecker. When I ran outside again the bird was still there, allowing me to move closer still until I was no more than forty feet away. How thrilling to be so close to such a magnificent creature! For a long time I stood watching, marveling at the tremendous force applied by the head as it knocked into the wood. (How could it create such force without harming its brain?) He was working on a tree located on my land, but watching him work I felt like I was trespassing on his property.

When the bird finally flew away, I came forward to inspect the damage. The woodpecker had bored holes a full four inches into the trunk. There was evidence the bird had feasted; a few errant ant legs had been left behind.

How had that pileated woodpecker known that those insects were buried deep within that trunk? Smell? Instinct? Experience? Would he return to bore new holes? Could holes like that damage the tree or ultimately kill it? Sure enough, I was grateful to know the precise name of this bird, but that was only the beginning of what I wanted to know.

14 *Parting Shots*

**To me the greatest pleasure of writing is not
what it's about, but the inner music that words make.**

Truman Capote

Writing involves putting the right words in the right order to create the effect you want. Working writers in every field and specialization delight in playing with language in order to create new effects—pyrotechnics. The more comfortable you are playing with language, the better you're able to create sentences with juice and pizzazz.

The strategies put forth in this book involve matters of craft, but not in the cold sense of the word. I am talking about doing whatever it takes to make your words come alive. I envision each of these pyrotechnics as a free pass for young writers to get out of jail, goof around, spread their wings, and, just maybe, come up with something that no one has ever done before.

In this book I have tried to show that writers create sentences using the ear as much as the eye. We have examined a range of pyrotechnics, but some don't fit into any particular category. Recently while reading a sports column in the *Boston Globe* written by Dan Shaughnessy, I came across this description of DeJuan Blair, a basketball player from the University of Pittsburgh. Blair weighs 265 pounds; Shaughnessy explained that Blair's large derriere is effective in keeping other players away from the basket. He wrote, "His upside is his backside" (2009).

As we come to the backside of this book I find myself doing the salmon dance, swimming back to the place where my life began.

Pease porridge hot,
Pease porridge cold,
Pease porridge in the pot nine days old . . .

Once upon a time my life was saturated in language play. And you know what? My days still begin that way. The first thing I see when I open the *Boston Globe* every morning is the weather forecast in the upper right-hand corner. Whoever writes those weather headings has a mischievous streak because he or she always manages to incorporate a tasty bit of wordplay: an allusion, altered expression, double meaning, or playful pun:

Pall O'er Me, No
Half an Ice Day ("Windy and colder despite some sun . . .")
Sunny Side Up
March Gladness
Pluck of the Airish (on St. Patrick's Day)
Cruel Twist of State ("Temperatures will plunge . . .")
A Pall Loose, Ah
Sun Sets in the Wet ("Rain will move in later . . .")
The Showers That Be
Fog Gone It
Sunny Being Sunny (a play on "Manny [former Boston Red Sox outfielder Manny Ramirez] Being Manny")

On March 23, 2009, stalwart Red Sox pitcher Curt Schilling announced his retirement. The temperatures in Boston would trend warmer that day. The next day the weather heading in the *Globe* read simply: Farewell Chilling.

It tickles me to see prime real estate in a serious newspaper given over to such whimsy. But I'll tell you this: it definitely helps get me in the mood to write. That little jolt of language play is all it takes to kick-start my motor as I leave the dock and venture out into the rollicking lake of language where I live.

15 *Questions and Answers*

Q: *Is the main purpose of using these pyrotechnics to make the writing livelier?*

A: It's one of them. But the ultimate goal is to make the writing work better. Writing is a matter of putting words in a particular order to create the effect you want. The pyrotechnics described in this book give the writer a new set of tools to help create the desired effect.

Q: *It sounds like you are saying that when it comes to teaching kids about language, teachers should teach experimentation and play instead of conventions.*

A: No. Imagine this continuum for teaching students about words/language:

Conventions ——————— **Exploration**
(Rules, definitions)   (Play, experimentation)

Where should teachers direct our energies?

I say: both.

I don't suggest that we should abandon teaching traditional language content (grammar, spelling, usage, vocabulary, etc.). But I do urge teachers to make language play a bigger part of the writing curriculum. The best way to ensure that kids learn about language is to encourage them to roll up their sleeves, appropriate it, make it their own. We need to promote play over mastery—at least at first—and recognize that for many young learners play is the surest means toward mastery.

Q: *Whenever you teach a craft lesson is there a danger of oversimplifying writing, turning writing into a recipe?*

A: Yes. Creating an effective piece of writing is more than adding the right literary spices: a dash of alliteration, a half-cup of metaphors, a tablespoon of not-too-ripe onomatopoeia. As the wicked witch in *The Wizard of Oz* put it: These things must be handled delicately. We must make sure that none of us lose sight of the real goal—to create stronger, more effective writing that fulfills the desired purpose. The language play should never be done for its own sake, but rather should serve the story as a whole.

Q: *Whenever I introduce a new writing strategy my students tend to overdo it. What if that happens with these pyrotechnics?*

A: Expect that they *will* overdo it. For example, once you allow them to use sentence fragments in a story, you'll find fragments all over their writing for a few weeks. That's a typical stage in learning—we all tend to overuse a skill or strategy immediately after we learn it. Eventually students will learn to integrate it appropriately and strategically, and it will become just one more tool in their repertoire as writers.

Q: *You are advocating inventing words and breaking the rules of sentences. But isn't there some value in linguistic conformity?*

A: Yes. As a matter of fact, Tom Romano told me a revealing story that touches on this very issue. He and his wife took their three-year-old daughter to a plaza in Italy with a lovely fountain. When Mariana saw it, the child got very excited.

"Jumping water!" she exclaimed.

Later Tom related this story at an inservice workshop. The teachers murmured appreciatively.

"That is precocious for a three-year-old," one teacher allowed. "But if your daughter is still saying 'jumping water' when she's eleven, well, they'll sign her up for remedial help."

It's a fair point. At some point Mariana should know that the correct word is *fountain*. Part of a teacher's job is to make sure that all the students learn a common vocabulary for the world around them. It can certainly be argued that linguistic conformity is a legitimate goal and integral to a smoothly functioning society.

But there can be a cost to this, too. When this idea is taken to extremes we end up with lockstep uniformity. In our rush to establish a common vocabulary and make sure students are "at grade level," I fear that we are devaluing the richness and diversity of their language, eliminating what might be fresh and interesting if it is even slightly out of the box or irregular.

Q: *Wouldn't it be better for teachers to spend precious time and energies encouraging students to work instead of play?*

A: I'll answer that question in two ways. On a philosophical level, I believe that those two terms may be more similar than you might think. Imagine a jazz trio as the musicians riff off each other, improvising, trying to concoct a new variation on a familiar melody. Or picture Michael Jordan flying through the air, his tongue hanging out, trying to decide at the last moment if he should pass to a teammate or flip the ball up to the basket. Are these people working or are they playing? It seems to me that, at the highest level, play and work become almost indistinguishable.

On a practical level, I believe it comes down to engagement. When kids play, they are engaged. And when they are genuinely engaged, they learn. I am a constructivist. Kids learn by actively doing—not by having things done to them.

Q: *Your book puts a lot of emphasis on puns and double meanings. Why?*

A: For one thing, it's a very accessible kind of language play. Puns rain down on students every day: on TV, in ads, on bumper stickers and license plates, and in songs. Since they are so ubiquitous, puns are natural portals for helping students to experiment with language. One of the unexpected pleasures in writing this book was being able to renew contact with James Heffernan, who was one of my English professors when I was at Dartmouth.

"The pleasures provoked by wordplay are similar to those provoked by figurative language," Heffernan said. "Both involve a double play, and it's always fun to see two things being done at once, different meanings crossing at one verbal intersection. Wordplay subverts the assumption that every word has a fixed and determinate reference shared by all speakers of that language. But many words, of course, have more than one meaning, and Lewis Carroll (among many others) had a fine time with this plurivocity."

Q: *Do metaphors and similes fall into the category of pyrotechnics? When I talk to my students about similes during our poetry unit, their eyes seem to glaze over. Help!*

A: Metaphors and similes certainly are pyrotechnics, but in many classrooms these terms have been overexposed. That's unfortunate. They should be front and center in any writer's toolbox because they are fundamental ways to create something new and memorable. Maybe we need to revisit the way we talk about these terms. And let's make sure students understand that metaphors and similes are not confined to poetry but can be used in every other kind of writing, as well.

Q: *Do you have any thoughts on how to help my students pick up on the power of metaphor?*

A: We need to share with our students examples of metaphors from literature, of course. We should also scour our classroom for student samples. Let them see their peers using them. And we should also share them from our own lives. It's my belief that the best metaphors are intensely personal.

When my son Robert was in third grade he scraped together thirty-five dollars for Christmas presents. That was a huge sum of money for him, but precious little for all the Christmas presents he needed to buy for our large family. My sister Kathy volunteered to take Robert shopping.

"The money I've saved is my robot," Robert observed to Kathy when they arrived at the mall. "Every time I buy a present, one part of the robot's body gets destroyed."

First Robert purchased a present for me: a blank notebook. As he handed over five dollars to the clerk, he cracked to Kathy, "Well, there goes an arm."

After buying a CD for his brother Adam, Robert sighed and muttered, "There goes a leg."

Later, when he bought drawing pencils for JoAnn, he told Kathy, "There goes the body." Soon all the money was gone.

That night at dinner, Kathy wanted a few minutes to eat and asked Robert if he might babysit her infant son for a half hour.

"I'll pay you," she told Robert.

This made his face brighten up.

"Hmm," he mused with a sly smile. "I see a robot, reconstructed."

Robert is nineteen now, but even today when he is a bit short of money I'll hear him remark: "I really need to rebuild my robot."

Q: *The administrators in my district seem to care about one thing only: test scores. Our faculty meetings are spent disaggregating test data, not my idea of a fun time. How can I reconcile teaching pyrotechnics with the grinding reality of tests?*

A: It may be that these pyrotechnics go against the current current. Curriculum mandates and standardized tests are a double whammy that have changed writing classrooms and, I'm afraid, not for the better. When I visit classrooms around the United States and abroad, it seems like real choice is disappearing. I am dismayed to see so much formulaic writing. This has impacted the energy level in the classroom. Lots of young writers—especially boys—seem turned off.

Sure, we want our students to be competent writers when they leave our classrooms. But this competence must come with voice. The language must have energy, juice. The pyrotechnics in this book can provide that spark. Personally, I would trade ten error-free essays that put me to sleep for one written with genuine voice and bold, striking language. Even if it contains a fragment. Or other error.

My niece, Rebecca, has a sign in her kitchen that reads, "Love is like bread—it has to be made fresh every day."

Writing is like that. Teaching, as well. You cannot fall back on any paint-by-number scheme. You have a responsibility to renew the language every time you write—and every time you teach.

CRAFT

LESSONS

16

Pyrotechnics Craft Lessons for Young Writers

In this chapter I'll offer specific lessons language teachers might use to bring pyrotechnics to young writers in a lesson format. It is my intention that these lessons be situated within a writing workshop in which a wide range of other lessons are taught: habits of writers, processes writers typically find helpful, strategies, skills, and so forth. (See *Writing Workshop: The Essential Guide* [Fletcher and Portalupi 2001] for more information on how to set up and manage a writing workshop.) While these craft lessons could fit naturally into the mini-lesson portion of a workshop, they could also provide rich fodder for conversation during a writing conference or even during reading workshop.

I am no fan of scripted curriculum, but I remind myself that I learned how to confer with students by following Shelley Harwayne through dozens of New York City classrooms and studying the various ways she conferred with young writers. Later, when it was my turn to confer with students, I would emulate those Shelley-conferences, often "borrowing" her language word for word. I offer the specific language in these lessons as a starting place, a discussion point only, and encourage you to alter/personalize these lessons as soon as you feel ready to do so.

Follow the pacing that feels right for you. Some of the lessons could easily be slowed down and spread over two days, depending on how deep a teacher wants to go.

These lessons draw on particular texts. Where possible I have also included a second text to use as an alternative in case the primary text is not available. In some cases, the lesson draws on a model that can be found in one of the appendixes.

Craft lessons should not be taught randomly or as part of some arbitrary preset sequence but as a result of careful watching. By observing your students, you can get a pretty good idea if they are ready to learn about a particular pyrotechnic. Pay attention to

* students noticing examples of wordplay during their reading,
* the appearance of language play in students' natural speech,
* and everyday classroom events.

"Just today I heard two fifth graders playing with puns at the water fountain," says Suzanne Whaley, a reading teacher at Bailey's Elementary School in Falls Church, Virginia. "Now's the time to teach them a craft lesson on puns!"

Note for Primary Teachers

Pyrotechnics represent a kind of "stretch language" that will be a challenge for children in kindergarten through grade two, particularly for those whose first language is not English. The first eight lessons have been written to be age-appropriate for primary students, but it might be wise to keep these guidelines in mind as you begin.

* *Consider your timing.* The best time of the year to teach pyrotechnics to primary students is probably *not* September or October! It might be wise to wait until later in the year (after January 1) when students have begun to hit their strides as writers.
* *Tap the power of talk.* These lessons could provide rich fodder for conversations about the various ways writers play with words and why this can strengthen a piece of writing.
* *Make time for oral "guided practice."* Many of these craft lessons provide an opportunity for kids to "turn and talk" during the lesson itself, a time for students to verbally try out the strategy before they go off to write.
* *Teach writing during reading.* Typically, craft lessons provide rich content for the mini-lesson part of the writing workshop. But with primary children, these lessons could also be taught during a read-aloud or shared reading.

(Some, such as "Highlighting a Word by Making It BIGGER," could be taught in both.) Noticing and naming these pyrotechnics are crucial first steps toward using them intentionally.

* *Be patient.* Primary children will probably need a great deal of *ebbing* (sowing seeds, marinating, priming the pump) before they are ready to *flow*, that is, try out these ideas in their writing.

Each of these lessons represents a pyrotechnic that could easily be overused. Don't be surprised if students do overuse them, at first. In the long run we want to empower students to decide if, when, and how to use these strategies. When that happens, these pyrotechnics will have become another part of their repertoire as writers.

Highlighting a Word by Making It BIGGER

Discussion

While we want primary writers to know the conventions of sentences (a capital at the beginning, a period at the end, etc.), we also want to encourage them to be playful when it suits the meaning of their story or poem. This lesson puts forth an easy way for primary writers to do so. This strategy could be followed up by a similar one—how an author might make a word smaller to differentiate it from the rest of the text and make it stand out in the reader's mind.

How to Teach It

Most times we write regular old sentences, but sometimes writers decide to give the reader a little surprise. When we want to focus in on one word, when we really want to highlight it, we can write it bigger than all the others. We can write the word bigger plus write it in capital letters.

I'm going to read a book where the author does this. Watch carefully. When you see a word that looks like it's extra large, raise your hand, and I'll put a sticky note on that page. Later we'll go back and talk about it. *(Read one of the suggested texts. As you read and kids raise their hands, put a sticky note next to the enlarged words.)*

Let's look at a few of these places where the author made the words really big. Why do you think the author did this? *(Discuss. As an alternative, read the text without kids looking at it. "When you hear a word the author thought was important, raise your hand." Then look at the text and see how the word was printed.)*

Authors "blow up" certain words to draw attention to them. You can do this in your own writing. As you're writing, or when you reread what you've written, think of a word that is very important. That's the one you want to blow up. Supersize it! You could make it larger, you could write it in capital letters, and you could make it darker. Good luck!

Resource Material

No, David! by David Shannon
I Stink! or *I'm Dirty!* by Kate McMullan

K–2 | *Inventing Words*

Discussion

Inventing words is the ultimate in language play. This lesson issues a generous invitation to students to make up their own words. If students try this in their writing, you might follow up by asking why they chose the particular word they invented (sound? humor?) and why it is important to their story.

How to Teach It

Have you ever had a brand new box of crayons? Some boxes have sixty-four different colors. That's a lot. But sometimes, even with all those crayons, there's one color you really want that's not in your box.

That happens with words, too. The dictionary holds thousands and thousands of words. But once in a while the word you want doesn't exist. When this happens, writers do something that's pretty amazing. Abracadabra: they invent it!

Remember the book *Chicka Chicka Boom Boom*? *(Show students.)*

In this book we find lots of regular words, but some of the words are not. For instance, the title says *Chicka Chicka*. Do you think *chicka* is in the dictionary? Let's look it up. No, it's not there.

Later in the book it says, "skit skat skoodle doot." Do you think *skoodle* is a real word? Nope, the authors invented that word, too. Why do you think they invented those words? *(Discuss. Kids might suggest that the words are both fun to say, or have a pleasing sound, or are just silly/funny.)*

A word like *skoodle* adds to the music of the book. And Bill Martin Jr. and John Archambault aren't the only authors to make up a word. Dr. Seuss invented dozens of them. *(Share a few invented words from "The Sneetches.")*

As you write today, I invite you to try inventing a new word and using it in your story. Have fun—let your imagination go wild. I can't wait to see what you come up with.

Resource Material

Chicka Chicka Boom Boom by Bill Martin Jr. and John Archambault
Dictionary
The Sneetches and Other Stories by Dr. Seuss
A Bargain for Frances by Russell Hoban

Using Words That Imitate the Sounds They Describe   K–2

Discussion

The rain pitter-patters on the window. Words like that imitate the sounds of the words they describe. This concept is well within the reach of primary children. If this were my class I might mention the word *onomatopoeia* in a playful way, not as something you expect them to remember.

How to Teach It

There are certain special words that make the same sound as the ones they describe. The *boom* of thunder. The *crack* of the bat. The *buzzing* of bees. Let's say that word together: *buzzing*. Can you hear the bee sound? That's made by the two *z*'s in the middle of the word.

There's a creature called the cuckoo bird. They gave the bird that name because of the sound it makes: coo-coo!

There's a fancy word for words that imitate the sounds they make: *onomatopoeia*. If anyone can spell it, well, you're an amazing speller!

Authors often use onomatopoeia in their stories and poems. Remember when we read *The Great Fuzz Frenzy*? Let's look at the first few pages. (*Read aloud the first few pages up to the word* plunk.)

What words did we hear that make the sound they are describing? (*Kids will point out* boink, thump, rumble, *and* plunk. *You might repeat those words with your class, saying them out loud to reinforce the sounds.*)

Can you think of some other words that make the sound they are describing? (*List on a chart words such as* bang, tap, tweet, hiss, crunch, crackle, pop, moo, jingle, gurgle, roar.)

Today you might want to try one of these words—a word that makes its own sound—when you're writing. It's a good way to allow the reader to really hear what's happening in your story.

Resource Material

The Great Fuzz Frenzy by Janet Stevens and Susan Stevens Crummel
I Stink! by Kate McMullan
Chart with paper and marker

K–2	*Making Lively Comparisons*

Discussion

Comparing one thing to another is an excellent way to lift the quality of primary writing. A comparison allows the young writer to make a familiar topic more interesting by "borrowing" the qualities of something new and exotic. Comparisons help the reader think about something in a new way. The goal of this lesson is to raise students' awareness. Although it draws on picture books that use similes rather than metaphors, the distinction is unimportant at this level. It's enough to help students get the feel for comparing one thing to another.

How to Teach It

Writers try to describe something so a reader could really picture it: "On my first high dive, my belly felt so nervous."

One way to make your description stronger is to compare one thing to another: "On my first high dive, my belly felt like there were a million tiny firecrackers exploding in there." The writer compared the feeling in her belly—when it tickles—to firecrackers inside her tummy!

Let's read a book where the author uses a lot of comparisons. *(Read one of the books and lead a brief discussion.)*

This book had many comparisons. Which ones stuck in your mind? *(You might want to make a T-chart with the heading Actual Event/Thing/Feeling on the left and Lively Comparison on the right.)*

Today when you write you might try comparing one thing to another. You could try this when you're describing a person, a place, an object, or a feeling. Try to be as specific as possible. Instead of just writing "When my mom was pregnant, her belly got big," you could write, "When Mom was pregnant, her belly got as big as a ball." But the reader still might wonder: what kind of ball? A football? Baseball? Golf ball? Your description would be even stronger if you wrote, "When Mom was pregnant, her belly got as big as a beach ball." Now the reader can really picture it.

Resource Material

My Dog Is as Smelly as Dirty Socks: And Other Funny Family Portraits by Hanoch Piven
Quick as a Cricket by Audrey Wood

Exploring Expressions

Discussion

The literalness of primary students is legendary. Here we expose young writers to this more abstract kind of language. The goal here is awareness. You might extend this lesson by having your students go on an "Expression Hunt" for a few days. Make an ongoing class list that kids can add to as they find expressions in read-alouds or conversation.

How to Teach It

Has your mother or father ever said something like this?

> "Keep an eye on your little brother."
> "Don't put your head in the sand!"
> "Get your ducks in a row."

When a person says something like that we call it an expression. An expression is a team of words that work together. This word-team communicates an idea though not exactly what each word says. Let's say your mother says, "Grab your umbrella—it's raining cats and dogs!"

What does she mean? She doesn't mean that cats and dogs are falling from the sky! She's using an expression that means it's raining hard.

Expressions are great to use in writing because they can make your story more interesting. You find lots of them in books. Let's read a book that's full of expressions. In fact, I think we'll find one on just about every page. (Read Butterflies in My Stomach. After you finish reading it, discuss with the class. Invite them to share which expressions they liked and why they found them funny. You might list a few favorites on a chart.)

Can anyone think of an expression that someone in your family, or someone you know, has said? (Invite students to share.)

Expressions are another great tool to make your writing stronger and more interesting. Let me know if you decide to use an expression in your writing today.

Resource Material

Butterflies in My Stomach and Other School Hazards by Serge Bloch
Ve Lo Que Dices/See What You Say by Nancy Maria Grande Tabor. A great book for explaining English idioms to Spanish speakers.

| K–2 | *When Writers Refer to Something Outside the Story* |

Discussion

Although most primary children probably will not use allusions in their writing, there is value in immersing children in language-rich read-alouds. By reading from these texts frequently, and quoting from them, you build a pool of shared texts. Students may begin making reference to them in their conversation and, perhaps in later years, in their writing. Note: allusions can often be found in the illustrations of picture books.

How to Teach It

When writers are making their stories they sometimes use a trick. They may mention something or someone that we all know about: a book, a movie, a place, or a famous person. They sneak it into the story, and it makes the writing more interesting for the reader.

I'm going to read a book. Pay close attention as I do. Let's see if this book makes us think of another story you have heard before. *(Read* Goldilocks Returns.*)*

Did this book make you think of another story? *(Share. Kids will probably mention* Goldilocks and the Three Bears.*)*

You can do this yourself when you write. Let's say you want to describe the sound made by a really big person—your father, uncle, or big brother—as he's coming down the stairs. You could write, "While I was watching TV, I suddenly heard King Kong pounding down the stairs."

When you write that, most readers will understand that it's not actually King Kong, but a big, heavy person who sounds like him.

Or let's say you want to describe what it was like the first time you met your new teacher. You might write, "When he came into our classroom, everybody stopped talking and froze, as if Barack Obama himself had walked in."

Resource Material

Goldilocks Returns by Lisa Campbell Ernst
Piggie Pie! by Margie Palatini

Putting On a Mask

Discussion

This lesson is about personification: giving inanimate objects human qualities. This concept can easily be introduced by tapping into children's familiarity with pretend play. It might be wise to have modest expectations as to how far kids take this idea in their writing.

How to Teach It

Has anyone in this class ever put a white sheet over your head and pretended that you were a ghost? Have you ever pretended you were a puppy, a dinosaur, or maybe a superhero? *(Quick share.)*

Writers often do a similar thing. Instead of writing about a topic, they actually become the thing they are writing about: "I am a hailstone. If you find a sparkly diamond on the grass after a summer storm, that's me. I don't cost even one penny, but catch me quick before I melt away."

In *I Stink!* the author becomes the thing she's writing about. Let's see how she does it. *(Read* I Stink! *It's even better if students are already familiar with it.)*

In this book, we hear the garbage truck talking to us. What is he like? *(Share. You might point out that at one point the garbage truck says, "Did I wake you? Too bad!")*

I invite you to try this today and become the thing you are writing about. You've really got to use your imagination. Close your eyes and imagine what it would be like if you were the wind. Or the sun. Or an elephant.

Here's one last tip. You want to take on a certain kind of personality. Think of what you're writing about and decide: Should you be shy? Bossy? A know-it-all? Sweet and nice? I'll be interested to see if anyone tries this in your writing and, if you do, maybe you'd be willing to share with the rest of the class.

Resource Material

I Stink! by Kate McMullan
Barn by Debby Atwell

| K–2 | |

Using Words That Have Two Meanings

Discussion

The goal of this lesson is simply to make students aware that certain words or expressions have two meanings and, perhaps, to start playing with this idea in their writing. This is an early way to introduce primary children to the concept of puns.

How to Teach It

Okay, let me tell you a very short story. A little boy and his family all go to a cookout. His uncle is grilling hamburgers, hot dogs, and chicken. Everybody is hungry. A dog has been running around. Finally the dog stops and sits, panting, trying to get his breath.

"Now that's what I call a hot dog!" the little boy says.

Ha! This made everybody laugh because this boy just made a joke. *Hot dog* can mean two things: it's the food you eat, but it's also the overheated dog.

Sometimes writers will do this—use a word that means two things at the same time. That's called a *pun*. Writers do this for two reasons: to make the reader laugh, but also to make the reader think.

Let's read together a poem that has lots of words with two meanings. *(Read "Where Can You Find a New Nose?" Invite students to join in reciting the recurring refrain.)*

What words did you find in this poem that mean two things? *(Discuss. You might create an anchor chart, showing two meanings of the same word: human tongue and the tongue in a shoe, human ear and ear of corn, etc.)*

Using a word with two meanings is a good way to make your story more interesting. I'll be curious to see if anybody decides to try this in your writing.

Resource Material

"Where Can You Find a New Nose?" by Ralph Fletcher (Appendix J). Recopy this poem on a chart, or blow it up large enough for students to see.
Gimme Cracked Corn and I Will Share by Kevin O'Malley

Experimenting with Puns

Discussion

The goal here is to expose students to words and sayings that have multiple meanings. It's a bonus if they actually begin to experiment with puns in their writing. Note: in addition to books, puns can often be found in unlikely places, such as printed on wooden Popsicle sticks!

How to Teach It

Does anybody know what a pun is? *(Share.)*

Yes! A pun can be defined as similar words or phrases—or even one word with two meanings—that are deliberately confused to make a joke or play on words. For instance:

To write without a pencil is pointless. *(Have this sentence printed on a chart.)*

You may or may not find this funny, but it is a pun. *Pointless* has two meanings. The obvious meaning of *pointless* is that there's no point to it. But there's also another meaning. You literally cannot write something with your pencil when the point is broken off, right? So the sentence works both ways. Here are some other puns. *(Write sentences on chart.)*

I wondered why the ball was getting bigger. Then it hit me!
That rock is gneiss, but don't take it for granite.
What happened to a boy who drank 8 Cokes? He burped 7-Up.

(Discuss. Invite students to share their own examples.)
Puns involve double meanings, and that's why they can be funny.

This book, *Punished!* is about a boy who goes to the library and meets a mysterious old man who sprinkles magic dust on him. After that, the boy can't help speaking in puns. Let's read some of it. Pay attention so you can tell me what puns and double meanings you noticed. *(Read from pages 16–23 from* Punished! *Then make time to share. Be prepared to go back and find the page with the exact wording.)*

Think about puns. You might want to collect some puns in your writer's notebook. Or you might want to try including a pun in your writing.

Resource Material

Punished! by David Lubar

3–4

Using Alliteration in Storywriting

Discussion

Alliteration is the name for the literary technique where the initial sounds of particular words are repeated: "It floods the clam flats with lonely lunar light" (Fletcher 2003). Examples can be found in every genre of children's literature. The goal is to help students get a feel for what it feels like to read—and write—with their ear.

How to Teach It

Writers sometimes choose words in a sentence so the beginning sound is repeated several times in a row: "in the misty moisty morning."

Do you hear all the *m* sounds? That technique is called alliteration. Poets use alliteration, but other writers do, too—even nonfiction writers.

I'm going to read *Amos & Boris*, a book by William Steig. As I do, raise your hand when you hear a sound repeated within a sentence. *(Read* Amos & Boris. *When a student raises his/her hand, put a sticky note to mark that page.)*

Many of you heard places where the initial word sounds were repeated. On the first page we can find two examples: "surf sounds" and "bursting breakers." Why do you think William Steig did this? *(Discuss.)*

Writers pay attention not just to what a sentence means but also to how it sounds. Using alliteration is one way to call attention to a phrase and fix it into the reader's mind. It can add rhythm and make the writing more musical. Of course, this is one of those ideas that you don't want to overuse. You choose when and if you want to use it.

"Let's do one together. First we'll brainstorm a list of adjectives that begin with *w*. Pick two or three that go together and share them with the person next to you. *(Make time for students to share.)*

I invite you to experiment with alliteration today when you're writing. Here's how you might do it. If you're describing storm winds, try to think of an adjective with the *w* sound: *wailing winds*. Or you could try to think of a verb with the same sound: The *winds walloped* the coastal town. I'll be curious about what you come up with.

Resource Material

Amos & Boris by William Steig

The Great Fuzz Frenzy by Janet Stevens and Susan Stevens Crummel

Inventing Words

Discussion

This lesson invites students to throw caution to the wind and invent their own words. You might follow up this lesson in individual writing conferences, asking the students how they invented a particular word and how it functions in the story.

How to Teach It

Have you ever seen one of those monster dictionaries with about two thousand pages? There sure are a lot of words in there! But here's a funny thing: even with all those words sometimes a writer still can't find the exact one he or she wants. When that happens, writers make up their own word.

Little kids like to invent words, for example, a toddler who calls his favorite blankie his *rashmatag*. Have you, or anyone you know, ever invented a word? *(Share.)*

Writers often invent words. Dr. Seuss sure did it, many times.

In Andrew Clements's novel *Frindle*, the main character starts calling his pen his frindle. His teacher doesn't like that, but she can't stop the idea from spreading among the other students. Soon all the kids are saying frindle instead of pen.

Can you think of any other books you've read where the author invented a word? *(Share. Kids might mention the Harry Potter books.)*

I'm going to read a short section from *Marshfield Dreams: When I Was a Kid*. *(Read "Snicking Up the Rug.")*

In this author's family, his mother invented that word *snick*. It's a funny little word, and kind of fun to say: snick.

Inventing a new word for your writing is fun and imaginative, plus it's a nifty way of adding a dose of surprise to your story. (Of course, if you invent *too* many words your readers might get confused.) If you're intrigued by this idea, go ahead and try it in your writing today. See if you can invent a word to make your story more interesting.

Resource Material

Frindle by Andrew Clements
"Snicking Up the Rug" from *Marshfield Dreams: When I Was a Kid* by Ralph Fletcher (Appendix K)

3–4

Using Hyperbole for Dramatic Effect

Discussion

Hyperbole is a technique that kids use naturally when they speak. By their own admission, many students are drama queens (and kings) who often use overheated, exaggerated language to get attention. Here we ask students to consider experimenting with hyperbole. This technique can be used to emphasize a point and add voice to a piece of writing.

How to Teach It

You may remember a time when you got out of the water, shivering, and cried, "Quick, give me a towel! I'm freezing!"

Of course, you weren't really freezing. That was an exaggeration you used to get people to pay attention. That kind of exaggeration is called hyperbole, and it's something we all use at one time or another.

> The line outside the cafeteria stretched for miles.
> My backpack weighs a ton.
> I wanted to hang with my friends, but Dad gave me a million chores.

Hyperbole is a deliberate exaggeration or extravagant statement. It is a kind of expression or figure of speech not intended to be taken literally. This kind of exaggeration can also be useful when you write. Writers use hyperbole to emphasize a point, add dramatic voice, and inject humor into the writing.

Let's look at this poem, "Beach Baby." *(See Appendix L. Read the poem out loud.)*

As I read it again, see if you notice examples of hyperbole. *(Read and discuss. Kids may mention the ten-thousand-pound soaked diaper and the "baby so giant she blocks out the sun.")*

Whether you're working on a poem, nonfiction, or fiction, please consider using hyperbole to add a little oomph to your writing.

Resource Material

"Beach Baby" by Ralph Fletcher (Appendix L)
It Figures! Fun Figures of Speech by Marvin Terban

Using Repetition for Emphasis

Discussion

Certainly we don't want to encourage a young writer to be redundant, but deliberate repetition is an excellent way to emphasize an important part of the writing by letting that word or phrase echo or linger in the reader's ear.

How to Teach It

Let's take a look at *The Sandman* by Ralph Fletcher, illustrated by Richard Cowdrey. In this picture book we're going to find one place where the language gets repeated. (*Read* The Sandman. *Halfway through the book Tor must return to the dragon's lair to fetch another dragon scale. Tor realizes he must wait until the dragon has fallen into a deep sleep. You might want to make copies of the following paragraph or reprint it on a large chart.*)

> *The Sandman wanted to grab the scale right away, but he didn't dare. He waited until the dragon's red eyes closed. He waited until only smoke drifted from the dragon's great nostrils. He waited until its breaths came slow and easy. He waited a half hour more until he was absolutely certain the dragon was fast asleep.*

I'm sure you noticed the repetition on this page. Usually it's a bad idea to begin one sentence after another in the same way, but that's exactly what the author did here. Why do you think he did so? (*Make time for students to share their thinking.*)

The repetition of "He waited" does several things. It takes a string of sentences and connects them, links them together. It builds suspense by creating a "hot spot" that makes the reader linger on a dangerous part of the story.

If you like this idea you might try some repetition today in your own writing. Start by identifying a crucial part of the story. Then select a few words and repeat them a few times in successive sentences. I'll be curious to see what you come up with.

Resource Material

The Sandman by Ralph Fletcher (paragraph photocopied or reprinted on a large chart)

Amos & Boris by William Steig

3–4

Using Expressions for Humorous Effect

Discussion

Expressions (or idioms) constitute important tools in all kinds of communication. Here we ask kids to get a feel for expressions in a humorous context.

How to Teach It

Imagine that you approach your father by saying, "Dad, could I, well, I was wondering if . . . Do you think that, um, maybe I could . . . ?"

Finally he interrupts: "Don't beat around the bush! Tell me what you want."

"Don't beat around the bush" is an expression or idiom. An expression is a team of words that works together. You need all the words as a group or cluster to understand what they mean.

I'm going to read *And the Dish Ran Away with the Spoon*, a book filled with expressions you might recognize. Pay attention to them. After we read it, we'll go back and talk about which ones you noticed. We'll think about why the authors chose to include those expressions in the story. *(Read And the Dish Ran Away with the Spoon. On the seventh page of text you'll find "a fork in the road," "we're in a jam," "I'll take a stab at it.")*

Okay, let's talk about which expressions you found. *(Discuss.)*

As I read this book I saw you guys smiling. That tells me that the authors used these expressions in a funny way. Why? You may have noticed that many of these expressions have double meanings.

Be thinking of expressions as you write today. You might want to experiment with them yourself. If you're describing an argument, you could write that it was "coming to a boil." If you're describing a super-strict teacher, you could say she "ran a tight ship." Have fun with it! All right. That's all she wrote! Happy writing!

Resource Material

And the Dish Ran Away with the Spoon by Janet Stevens and Susan Stevens Crummel
Private I. Guana by Nina Laden
Gimme Cracked Corn and I Will Share by Kevin O'Malley

Breaking Rules for Sentences

Discussion

Whoa, wait a sec: breaking the rules for sentences?!? I'm trying to get my students to learn them! Well, yes. But while the rules of usage and grammar are certainly important, they can also be confining and lead to mass-produced sentences of numbing uniformity. This lesson encourages students to experiment and see what they can do when they are given carte blanche to make their own rules.

How to Teach It

In school we are always trying to reinforce the idea that sentences must have a subject and a verb. But must they? Let's look at *The Relatives Came*, a picture book you may know written by Cynthia Rylant. *(Read book. If the students already know this book, you can turn immediately to the page in question.)*

Look at this page. This is when the relatives are driving home to Virginia, thinking of their dark purple grapes waiting for them. On the next page the author writes:

> *But they thought about us, too. Missing them. And they missed us.*

Here we have three sentences. The first one begins with *but,* which, technically, you're not supposed to do. Look at the second one: "Missing them." Is that a sentence? Who is missing them? No, that's a sentence fragment. The third sentence begins with the word *and*, which is another no-no. Three sentences and each one breaks a rule of grammar!

I wonder why Cynthia Rylant decided not to attach "Missing them" to the previous sentence: "And she thought about us, too, missing them." What does it do to the writing when those two words stand apart as a sentence fragment? *(Discuss.)*

Cynthia Rylant writes: "Missing them." By itself. That sentence fragment emphasizes that they will really be missed by their relatives.

Authors like Cynthia Rylant know that when you write, you don't always have to follow every rule about sentences. On occasion. You. Can. Break. Them. Selectively. I just did. Today I encourage you to try this. See what happens when you "color outside the lines." You might try using a fragment in your writing: a sentence with a subject but no verb, or a verb but no subject. Or a run-on sentence that goes on for an entire paragraph. Remember: the goal is to make your writing stronger, to inject a little surprise, to add voice, and to make it more interesting for the reader.

Resource Material

The Relatives Came by Cynthia Rylant
Gorky Rises by William Steig
The Great Fuzz Frenzy by Janet Stevens and Susan Stevens Crummel

3–4

Using Short, Snappy Sentences

Discussion

Helping students gain some control over their sentences is a big step toward making them stronger writers. Here we ask them to consider the effect of interspersing short sentences amidst longer ones.

How to Teach It

When you're building a Lego structure, do you always use the same-sized pieces? No. Sometimes you need a long piece; other times a short one will do the trick.

Writing is the same way. Not all the sentences you write should be the same length. I'm happy to see you write sentences that flow along for one or two lines. But sometimes a short, snappy sentence can add a lot of punch to your writing. Let's take a close look at this story. *(Read "Sledding Disaster," Version 1, Appendix O.)*

Notice the sentences in this story are all roughly the same length. In fact, if you count the words in the first three sentences you'll see that each one has eight words. There's nothing horribly wrong with these sentences; they do tell the story. But when *all* your sentences are the same length, they can start to sound boring and monotonous for the reader.

Let's look at a different version of this story. *(Read "Sledding Disaster," Version 2.)*

What's different about this story? *(Invite student responses.)*

There are some important differences here. In this version when the sled ride starts to change, the sentences start to change, too. Toward the end of this version, the author uses lots of short, snappy sentences. This creates excitement and tension. Something is going to happen!

Think of this as you write today. You probably don't want to use all short, snappy sentences in your writing, but a few of them really can add energy to your story.

Resource Material

"Sledding Disaster," Version 1 and Version 2 (Appendix O)
Enlarge, put on overhead, or make copies for students.

Using an Interjection Inside a Sentence

3–4

Discussion

An interjection is a word, phrase, or sentence that interrupts writing in order to express emotion. It has no particular grammatical relation to the sentence. The idea of interrupting your own writing is an appealing one for kids—plus, they learn punctuation in the process because the interjection is always set off from the sentence by punctuation; for example, a comma, an exclamation point, a dash, or set of parentheses.

How to Teach It

Has this ever happened to you? You are telling a story when suddenly you interrupt yourself in order to react or add new information. In a similar way, you can interrupt yourself when you write. Let's see how:

> Nobody could find the baseball until—ta da!—I pulled it out of my backpack.
> My sister kissed the swing set (how clueless was that?) and her lower lip immediately froze to the metal pole.
> Mom put me in charge of guarding the birthday cake. I went down to the basement for just a few seconds, but when I returned—horrors!—the dog was happily eating the cake.
> Irene pushed forward with all her strength and—*sloosh! thwump!*—she plunged downward and was buried (from *Brave Irene* by William Steig).

What did you notice about these sentences? *(Invite students to pair-share and discuss.)*

The part of the sentence in the middle—the interrupting part—is called an interjection. Notice that you use punctuation before and after it. How odd to find an exclamation point or question mark in the middle of a sentence!

One other thing—the interjection isn't connected to the rest of the sentence. Notice that the sentence reads just fine without the interjection. *(Read aloud the sentences minus the interjections.)*

An interjection is a great way to inject a jolt of energy into a humdrum sentence. And it's a useful way to make a side comment or react to what's going on. I invite you to try this yourself in your writing.

Resource Material

Sentences above printed on chart, or copied for students
Brave Irene by William Steig

5+

Inventing Words

Discussion

Encouraging student writers to invent a new word is a generous invitation for them to be expansive and playful with their vocabulary.

How to Teach It

There are about 200,000 words in common use in the English language. With all that, you'd think there would be plenty of words for every possible need and purpose, but people are always creating new ones: *ginormous, truthiness, blamestorming, earjacking* (when someone is eavesdropping on your conversation).

Sometimes a little kid will invent a word—calling a wheeled walker a *dillybobble*, for example—and use it so often it becomes part of the family's vocabulary. Can you think of any words invented in songs or ads? *(Share.)*

It's common for writers to invent words, too. Lewis Carroll made up words like *vorpal* and *slithy* in his poem "Jabberwocky." Dr. Seuss invented words like *snarggled, cruffulous,* and *smogulous* (all from *The Lorax*). In the Harry Potter books, J. K. Rowling invented the word *Quidditch* along with many others.

Let's look at a picture book, *Once Upon a Twice*, where the author has invented a bunch of new words. As I read, take note of the new words this author has created. You might even take out some paper or your writer's notebook so you can write them down. *(Read* Once Upon a Twice *or, if you don't have a copy of the book, refer to Appendix G, which contains the text of the first two pages of the book. Discuss.)*

Which invented words struck you? Let's try to imagine why the author might have created that word. What purpose does it serve? *(As students mention words they wrote down, go back to the text and reread that part so the word can be read in context.)*

Today I'm issuing this invitation: go forth and invent! If the spirit moves you, create a new word to fit your story. Your word might be a combination of two actual words or a completely new creation. Good luck!

Resource Material

Once Upon a Twice by Denise Doyen
Extract from *Once Upon a Twice* (Appendix G)
The Lorax by Dr. Seuss

Asking Questions to Engage the Reader

5+

Discussion

This lesson invites students to consider the usefulness of questions in engaging the reader. Because this technique invites the writer to address the reader directly, it can help amplify the voice.

How to Teach It

Do you know anyone who has ever sneaked a candy bar from a store or supermarket without paying for it? *(Brief discussion.)*

Let's stop and reflect on what just happened. See what I did? I asked you a question as a way to get you engaged and interested. Writers do that, too. Asking an intriguing question is a great way to grab the reader's attention.

Let's look at one student who did something like this in a piece he wrote. *(Read "Chocolate" by Max Gilmore, Appendix M. Ideally, you should duplicate it so students can have a copy.)*

What do you think? What parts did you especially like? *(Discuss. Students may mention the details, and the obsession with chocolate.)*

Did you notice that this writer uses questions to engage the reader? Take another look at the first paragraph. Max starts by asking a question. He does it again by asking "question fragments" that don't even have a verb—"The culprit?" "The victim?"

Max also uses questions in the last paragraph. *(Discuss. Kids might mention that in the last paragraph Max gives surprising answers to the questions he asks.)*

Asking the reader questions is a trick or strategy used by reporters, magazine writers, novelists. Today when you write, see if a well-placed question or maybe even several questions might help you draw in the reader.

Resource Material

"Chocolate" by Max Gilmore (Appendix M)

5+ *Trying Out a Pun*

Discussion

Kids are intrigued by puns because they want to be in on the joke. In third grade students are exploring puns, but by fifth grade you'll find them trying to include puns in their writing. We need to be generous with these early attempts; don't be surprised if they sound awkward or forced.

How to Teach It

I have a sentence that I'd like you to read.

Most people can't write poetry—they should leave it to the prose.

Get it? Maybe this isn't hysterically funny, but it is clever. You can read it as "leave it to the prose" or "leave it to the pros." It works both ways.

Let's do another one. Imagine an English boy sitting in history class.

"Nobody dared challenge the English empire," the teacher declares.

The student raises his hand. "But how about when the American colonies revolted?"

The teacher frowns. "Oh yes. Those revolting *colonies!"*

This is funny because *revolting* can also mean disgusting. These are puns. A pun is a play on words where the word means two things at once. Puns are like a double play, a two-for-one, a buy-one-get-one-free.

Sometimes a pun will have two words that aren't really the same but sound alike: "He drove his expensive car into a tree and found out how the Mercedes bends."

Have you heard any puns on TV shows, in commercials, or in movies? *(Invite students to share. If you have time, share some puns from J. Patrick Lewis's poetry, Appendix I.)*

Writers love to use puns to liven up their work and add a dash of humor. In the Harry Potter series, there is an alley named Diagon Alley, which is a pun for *diagonally*. Today as you write, think about including a pun in your writing if you have a chance to do so. Have fun with this. If anyone does use a pun, please let me know so we can share.

Resource Material

Puns cited above, written out on large chart paper
Poetry by J. Patrick Lewis (Appendix I)
The Xanth books by Piers Anthony

Playing with a Double Meaning

Discussion

While the double meaning may be a stretch for some students, it's a concept widely used in book titles (*Drop Dead Gorgeous*), TV (*Raising Cain*, the PBS special about boys), and advertising ("Nothing runs like a Deere").

How to Teach It

Most writers use clear, straightforward language. But sometimes a writer will use a word or phrase that can mean two things at the same time. Puns do that. Today we're going to talk about the double meaning, which is similar to a pun but without the humor.

Twilight Comes Twice is a poetic picture book. In the middle of it we find this page that reads:

> *Dawn slowly brightens*
> *the empty baseball field,*
> *polishing the diamond*
> *until it shines.*

Part of the reader's pleasure is discovering and considering the double meanings of "polishing the diamond."

Now let's take a look at a poem that does something similar. *(Read "Owl Pellets," Appendix N. If you have time, read it twice.)*

Notice any double meanings in this poem? It ends with the line "certain things are just about impossible to swallow," which refers to the owl but also to the boy who sees a girl he likes sitting with another boy.

A double meaning is a nifty thing that can make the reader think twice about what you're writing. It won't work for every story or poem, but it can be very effective, especially when used as an ending. Consider trying a double meaning in the piece of writing you're working on. Here's one tip: when you use a double meaning in your writing you don't want to explain it. Rather, leave room for the reader to figure it out.

Resource Material

Twilight Comes Twice by Ralph Fletcher
"Flying in the Face of Reason" by Rick Reilly (Appendix H)
"Owl Pellets" from *I Am Wings* by Ralph Fletcher (Appendix N)

5+

Using Allusion in Your Writing

Discussion

Allusion is a sufficiently complex notion that kids might need more than one exposure to grasp it. If you see value in this concept, make a note to revisit it later in the year. Be patient if students tend to make allusions to pop culture in their writing rather than literature.

How to Teach It

On a newspaper sports page I found this sentence:

Tim Wakefield is now within three weeks of his 43rd birthday, and it's time to wonder if, like [Benjamin] Button, he's aging backward.

This author is describing a baseball pitcher by comparing him to a character in a popular movie. This is an allusion: a reference to a book, character, event, TV show, or movie that you assume will be known to the reader. Making an allusion is a great way to describe something. It allows you to draw upon the ideas and emotions most people would have connected to what you're referring to, for example:

She was the light of my life, and I thought she felt the same way, but last summer the twin towers of our love came crashing down.

When it comes to using an allusion, the possibilities are limitless. You can try this in your writing. You might make an allusion to a myth, fairy tale, TV show, or play. You could describe a stingy character as a Scrooge or Grinch; you could describe a successful businesswoman by saying she has the Midas touch. Choose an allusion depending on what you want to say.

The substitute teacher stood at her desk, innocent as the captain of the Titanic *moments before it collided with the iceberg.*

An allusion like this creates a sense of doom or foreboding. Something bad is about to happen!

Resource Material

The Watsons Go to Birmingham—1963 by Christopher Paul Curtis (numerous allusions, including Jack Frost and *et tu, Brute*)
A Series of Unfortunate Events by Lemony Snicket

Experimenting with "Reversible Raincoat Sentences"

5+

Discussion

The sentence reversal is a rhetorical flourish that is a real showstopper. To prepare for this lesson, recopy the examples on large chart paper so kids can have a close-up view.

How to Teach It

When John F. Kennedy was president, his speechwriters sometimes wrote a special kind of sentence with two parts. The second part of the sentence reversed words taken from the first part: "Ask not what your country can do for you—ask what you can do for your country."

Calvin Trillin called these "reversible raincoat sentences" because, like some raincoats, they can be worn or used inside out. You've heard these before, and they really stick in your mind.

Let's try some together. "When the going gets tough . . ." *(Underline the words* going *and* tough.)

How could I write the second part of this sentence by reversing words taken from the first part? *(Allow students to finish this sentence: ". . . the tough get going.")*

Maybe you've heard that one before. How about this one? "We must master our fear . . ." *(Underline the words* master *and* fear.)

"We must master our fear or else fear will be our master."

Let's do one more: "It's important to live the life you love and . . ." *(Underline* live *and* love. *Then wait for students to respond.)*

". . . love the life you live." *(If you have time, share more examples from Appendix D.)*

Good. I think you're starting to get a feel for it. This technique isn't reserved for the professionals—you can try it out in your writing. Experiment and see what you come up with. Obviously, this kind of reversal won't always work, and it may not be appropriate for every piece you write, but it can be very effective. I'll be curious to see if any of the writers in here use this idea, either today or later in the year.

Resource Material

"Sentence Reversals" (Appendix D)

5+

Trying a 3-2-1 (or 1-2-3) String of Sentences

Discussion

We want students to realize that sentences do not exist in isolation but as part of a series, connected to what comes before and after. The goal here is to attune students to the cadence or musicality in a series of sentences.

How to Teach It

You write with the ear as well as the eye. Certainly, it's important to observe closely and create vivid images for the reader. But at the same time, writers try to create sentences that sound good, that flow together in a pleasing way.

One way to do that is to write three sentences that have a 3-2-1 rhythm. To do this you write one long sentence, then a shorter sentence, followed by the shortest sentence.

> *Some people take years and years before they decide what they want to do with their lives. Others need to go to college or grad school to figure it out. Not me.*

You can almost clap this out. The first sentence has twenty syllables, the second has sixteen, and the third has two. This kind of rhythm has a cumulative effect; it builds up. A long sentence followed by a shorter one sets us up for the ultrashort third one.

You can also do this in reverse to create a 1-2-3 cadence:

> *Chocolate. There are so many varieties to buy, it can feel overwhelming. All those neatly stacked rectangles in their pretty wrappers, each one staring up at you, beckoning, promising to make your dreams come true.*

Today when you write, think about the cadence of your sentences. See if a 3-2-1 or 1-2-3 cadence would create the rhythm you want. You might want to count syllables in each sentence. After you write the string of sentences, quietly read them aloud and listen to the rhythm.

Resource Material

Sentences cited above

RESOURCES

Pyrotechnics Glossary

Alliteration: the repetition of the initial sounds in two or more words. Writers use alliteration to make the sentences flow more easily, to reinforce a particular sound, and to fix that sound in the ear of the reader. Alliteration can be found in many children's books, including:

Shrek! and other picture books by William Steig

Piggie Pie! by Margie Palatini

The Great Fuzz Frenzy by Janet Stevens and Susan Stevens Crummel

Pignic: An Alphabet Book in Rhyme by Anne Miranda

Craft Lesson:

Using Alliteration in Storywriting (3–4) on page 114

Allusion: a reference, either direct or implied: "The field behind our house was as unspoiled as the Garden of Eden. And then the bulldozers arrived." (See Chapter 9.) Examples of allusion can be found in many children's books, including the Magic School Bus series by Joanna Cole and Bruce Degen.

Craft Lessons:

When Writers Refer to Something Outside the Story (K–2) on page 110

Using Allusion in Your Writing (5+) on page 126

Aphorism: a short saying that conveys a general truth, cleverly expressed. "*Believe nothing you hear, and only half of what you see*" (Mark Twain).

Assonance: the repetition of vowel sounds *inside* a series of words in a line or a sentence. For instance, listen to the series of short *i* sounds in this phrase: "the inquisitive fingers of the wind."

Referring to assonance and alliteration, the poet Robert Wallace said, "Their main value is the linking of sounds to thread lines together so they are tight and harmonious" (1991, 111).

For elementary school students, examples of assonance can be found in picture books by William Steig, for example, in *Amos & Boris*: "He thought a lot about the ocean . . ."

Middle and secondary students might look at Edgar Allan Poe's famous poem "Annabel Lee," which contains a succession of long *i* sounds:

> *And so, all the night-tide,*
> *I lie down by the side*
> *Of my darling—my darling—my life and my bride*

Foreshadowing: to hint at events that occur later in the book or story. There's a good example of foreshadowing in Jane Yolen's picture book *Encounter* (1996). The boy dreams of "three great-winged birds with voices like thunder." The next day his dream becomes true when he sees three "great-sailed canoes" approaching.

Homophone: two words that are pronounced the same way but differ in meaning. For example: "I just heard a grown-up groan up ahead!" Some useful books for teaching kids about homophones:
Dear Deer: A Book of Homophones by Gene Barretta
How Much Can a Bare Bear Bear: What Are Homonyms and Homophones? by Brian P. Cleary

Craft Lesson:
Using Words That Have Two Meanings (K–2) on page 112

Hyperbole: an exaggeration of something, used for emphasis: "My uncle shook my hand, his fist like a huge slab of roast beef."

Craft Lesson:
Using Hyperbole for Dramatic Effect (3–4) on page 116

Metaphor: a figure of speech in which two unlike things are compared:

> *Baby turtles emerge from eggs*
> *tucked beneath the blanket of sand*
> *where their mother left them. (Fletcher 2003)*

Many examples can be found in children's literature, including:
Owl Moon by Jane Yolen
Knots on a Counting Rope by Bill Martin Jr. and John Archambault
Kitten's First Full Moon by Kevin Henkes (for primary students)

Onomatopoeia: a word that sounds the same as, or similar to, what it represents. Words such as *plunk, crunch, splash, murmur, tap, crackle,* and *whoosh* can enhance description by bringing an auditory richness into a sentence. Suggested resources:
"Onomatopoeia," a poem by Eve Merriam
The Journey That Saved Curious George by Louise Borden. This picture book contains lovely examples of onomatopoeia, including "the flutter of pigeons" and "the quick rumble of taxis."
Secondary teachers might have students look at "Come Down, O Maid" by Tennyson, which concludes with these lines:

> *The moan of doves in immemorial elms,*
> *And murmuring of innumerable bees. (2008, 93)*

Galway Kinnell's poem "Burning the Brush Pile" has some memorable onomatopoeia:

> *I poured diesel all gurgling*
> *and hiccupping into the center of the pile. (2008, 21)*

Craft Lesson:
Using Words That Imitate the Sounds They Describe (K–2) on page 107

Oxymorons: two incongruous words that are used together. (See Appendix B.) An oxymoron involves a working contradiction, putting contradictory words side by side, often creating a dramatic, humorous, or ironic effect: *junk food, devilish nun, deafening silence.* While some oxymorons are obvious, others are a matter of opinion: *military intelligence.* Useful books for introducing oxymorons to students include:

Runny Babbitt: A Billy Sook by Shel Silverstein
Red Kayak by Priscilla Cummings (novel)
Punished! by David Lubar (see pages 41–59)

Note: sometimes a writer will create a phrase using two words that pull in opposite directions, for example, *perfumed lies* in a column by Leonard Pitts (*Miami Herald*, November 5, 2008). While not technically an oxymoron, this kind of wordplay creates a similar kind of tension that can be quite useful to a writer.

Palindrome: a word, phrase, or sentence that reads the same backward as forward; for example: "Able was I ere I saw Elba" (Napoleon). Suggested books:

Go Hang a Salami! I'm a Lasagna Hog! And Other Palindromes by Jon Agee
Palindromania! by Jon Agee
Mom and Dad Are Palindromes by Mark Shulman

Personification: a figure of speech that assigns human qualities, actions, or characteristics to an animal, object, place, or natural force. This technique allows a writer to humanize inanimate objects or nonhuman animals by allowing them to perform human actions:

Warm sunlight caressed her cheek.

The only sounds were the occasional complaints from the old wooden planks on the dock.

The dawn slowly pours the syrup of darkness into the forest. (Fletcher 1997)

For more examples, see the following:
I Stink! by Kate McMullan
I'm Dirty! by Kate McMullan

Craft Lesson:
Putting On a Mask (K–2) on page 111

Pun: a play on words in which a word or phrase is used to express two meanings at the same time. This is usually done to create a humorous effect: "The police were called to the day care center because one toddler was resisting a rest." (See Chapter 7.)

Craft Lessons:
Using Words That Have Two Meanings (K–2) on page 112
Experimenting with Puns (3–4) on page 113
Trying Out a Pun (5+) on page 124

Repetition: the use of a particular word or phrase more than once. Poets and song-writers have long known the value of repetition, but it is also useful when writing prose. By repeating a particular word, a writer can emphasize a particular part or create cohesion between phrases or sentences. There are many wonderful examples of repetition in William Steig's picture book *Amos & Boris* (1971):

> *Day and night he moved up and down, up and down, on waves as big as mountains, and he was full of wonder, full of enterprise, and full of love for life.*

As with all the other techniques in this book, students will need guidance when using repetition. Don't be surprised if they overuse it or need to be reminded that repeating for deliberate effect is not the same thing as being redundant.

Craft Lesson:
Using Repetition for Emphasis (3–4) on page 117

Rhyme: the repetition of similar sounds in two words. Rhyme's usefulness is not limited to poetry; it gives prose writers yet another way to animate a sentence by giving the ear something to grab on to: "The chief purpose of slang is to show you're one of the gang."

Some writers use internal rhyme—a rhyme within a sentence. One of my favorite lines in Kate McMullan's picture book *I Stink!* is this one: "No skunk ever stunk THIS BAD!"

Simile: a figure of speech in which one thing is compared to another using *like* or *as*. Suggested books:

The Cowboy and the Black-Eyed Pea by Tony Johnston

Quick as a Cricket by Audrey Wood

My Dog Is as Smelly as Dirty Socks and Other Funny Family Portraits by Hanoch Piven

Craft Lesson:

Making Lively Comparisons (K–2) on page 108

Spoonerism: a particular kind of language play where the initial sounds of two or more words are reversed for comic effect, for example, "Go and shake a tower." Or, "A well-boiled icicle." Suggested books:

Smart Feller Fart Smeller: And Other Spoonerisms by Jon Agee

Runny Babbit: A Billy Sook by Shel Silverstein

Molly Moon's Hypnotic Time Travel Adventure by Georgia Byng. In this middle-grade novel, Molly encounters a creature who speaks in spoonerisms.

Symbolism: the use of symbols or icons that carry particular meanings. Symbols are subjective; two people may interpret the same symbol differently. In *The Two of Them*, a picture book by Aliki, I interpret the ring that appears in the beginning of the book as a symbol of both the love between the girl and her grandfather and the circularity of time.

Understatement: to make something appear lesser or smaller than it actually is. Understatement is the opposite of hyperbole. Example: "Ross Pirelli was not the smallest kid in the senior class. He stood six foot five, weighing close to three hundred pounds." You can find many examples of understatement in *Peter Rabbit* by Beatrix Potter.

Wordplay: when the nature of the words used becomes an aspect of the work itself:

One misty, moisty morning,
When cloudy was the weather,
I chanced to meet an old man
Clothed all in leather.
He began to compliment,
And I began to grin,
How do you do?
And how do you do?
And how do you do, again?

Oxymorons

Act naturally
Advanced BASIC
Almost exactly
Alone together
American English
Authentic replica
Awfully good

Bad luck
Baked Alaska
Bittersweet
Black light
Blank expression
Business ethics
Butthead

Cardinal sin
Civil war
Classically modern
Clearly confused
Cold comfort
Conspicuous absence
Constant change
Cowardly lion

Criminal justice
Deafening silence
Death benefits
Definite maybe
Deliberate thoughtlessness
Down escalator
Dynamic equilibrium
Even odds
Exact estimate
Extensive briefing
Extinct life

Fairly dark
Forgotten memories
Found missing
Freezer burn
Fresh-frozen
Friendly fire
Front end
Fuzzy logic

Genuine imitation
Good grief
Great Depression

Guest host
Hell's Angels
Highly underestimated
Holy war
Homeless shelter
Hopelessly optimistic

Idiot savant
Ill health
Industrial park
Instant classic
Intense apathy

Job security
Jumbo shrimp

Least favorite
Light heavyweight
Liquid gas
Little giant
Live recording
Living dead
Loose tights
Loosely packed

Managed competition
Military intelligence
Minor crisis
Modern history

Natural additives
Noble savage
Nonalcoholic beer
Normal deviation
Nothing much
Numb feeling

Oddly appropriate
Old news
Only choice
Open secret
Original copy

Paid volunteer
Passive aggression
Peace force
Peacekeeper missile

Peace offensive
Plastic wood
Positively cynical
Pretty ugly
Pronounced silence

Random order
Real potential
Recorded live
Resident alien
Rock opera
Rolling stop

Safe sex
Safety hazard
Same difference
Second best
Serious fun
Short distance
Silent scream
Simply confusing
Soft rock

Spend thrift
Stand down
Still life
Still moving
Strangely familiar
Sure bet
Sweet sorrow

Terribly pleased
Tight slacks
True story

Unacceptable solution
Unbiased opinion
Uncrowned king

Virtual reality
Voluntary compliance

War games
Whole some
Working vacation

Expressions / Idioms

Apple of his eye

At the drop of a hat

Between a rock and a hard place

A bone to pick with you

Bone up on

Break a leg!

Bull in a china shop

Burn the midnight oil

Bury the hatchet

Bust my chops

Call a spade a spade

Caught red-handed

Chew the fat

A chip on his shoulder

Come down like a ton of bricks

Cut to the chase

Deep pockets

Deer in the headlights

Dig your heels in

Dodge a bullet

A double-edged sword

Down to the wire

An iron stomach

Kiss of death

Last nail in the coffin

Late bloomer

Make your blood boil

Method to your madness

Mover and a shaker

My way or the highway

Nature of the beast

Neck of the woods

New blood

No bed of roses

Nose out of joint

Once in a blue moon

On cloud nine

Open and shut

Over the top

Paint yourself into a corner

Paper tiger

Pipe dream

Play devil's advocate

Pull a rabbit out of your hat

Pushing up daisies

Put on the spot

Rags to riches

Read them the riot act

Real McCoy

Right off the bat

Ring true

Rock the boat

Roll with the punches

Rose-colored glasses

Rough around the edges

Ruffle his feathers

Sacred cow

Same old, same old

Sing for your supper

Six of one and a half dozen of the other

Skating on thin ice

Skin of my teeth

Speak of the devil

Splitting hairs

Start from scratch

Stick to your guns

Straw that broke the camel's back

Take the bull by the horns

Take the wind out of my sails

Take to the cleaners

Take with a grain of salt

Throw a wet blanket on

Throw down the gauntlet

Tongue in cheek

Walk on eggshells

Wet behind the ears

Whistling past the graveyard

White elephant

Wild goose chase

Yank my chain

Sentence Reversals

Calvin Trillin called these "reversible raincoat sentences."

Better a bear in the orchard than an Orchard in the bear. (Lynd Ward)

The strength of the wolf is in the pack, the strength of the pack is in the wolf.

Live the life you love, and love the life you live.

Ask not what your country can do for you—ask what you can do for your country. (President John F. Kennedy)

Mankind must put an end to war, or war will put an end to mankind. (JFK)

Let us never negotiate out of fear, but let us never fear to negotiate. (JFK)

What counts is not necessarily the size of the dog in the fight—it's the size of the fight in the dog. (Dwight D. Eisenhower)

In peace sons bury their fathers, but in war fathers bury their sons. (Croesus, sixth century BC)

In America, you can always find a party. In Soviet Russia, The Party can always find you! (Yakov Smirnoff)

You have seen how a man was made a slave; you shall see how a slave was made a man. (Frederick Douglass)

I flee who chases me, and chase who flees me. (Ovid)

Fair is foul, and foul is fair. (William Shakespeare)

Love makes time pass; time makes love pass. (French proverb)

Why do we drive on the parkway and park on the driveway? (Richard Lederer)

Rosie's Book of Sayings

Kim Stafford

A standard question in literary life is "What book most influenced you on your path to becoming a writer?" Many answers are possible, and the wonderful thing is that any book might be the most important at this moment. But overall, I realize I have an odd answer: The most important book for me was the first one I wrote—or helped to write. My parents called it *Lost Words*, and it was a compendium of the unusual things the four children in my family said when we were small, before we went to school. Both our parents were teachers, especially alert to adventures in language. And in his own daily writing practice, my father wrote down his favorites from our random utterance, and then he compiled them into a little book.

This book is important not because it is unusually brilliant. Every child I have met has unique insights and ways of expressing them. But *Lost Words* was *our* book. The ideas between its covers were our own philosophic landscape, and the language was our collective creation. My brother, Bret, my sisters, Kit and Barbara, and I together challenged each other to figure out the world, sentence by sentence, and question by question. Just because our parents were the teachers in the family did not mean we weren't all thinkers, writers, makers of culture. In *Lost Words*, democratic inclusion started in the family and became my career.

I cherish this record, and my own habit of writing down the daily wonders of conversation may have its source in this custom from home:

Kit looking at modern art: "These are just sort *of pictures, aren't they?"*

We bought a car last Monday. Yesterday Barbara was out beside it, tying it with a string—"So the wind won't blow it away."

Today, signing Kim's report card, I suggested writing "Incapable of doing any better." He rejoined that I should say, "Capable of doing much worse."

Remembering his friend after we moved away, Bret looked up at the sky and said, "Does our sky hook onto Donna's sky?"

Our mistakes with the language were so odd that our parents, ethnographers of our exotic tribe, simply wrote down our culture, our art, our errors and discoveries.

When my own daughter arrived, I took up this habit as listener, recorder. Little Rosemary, like all kids, had outrageous techniques for seeing the world, and she found ways the language could be bent to serve her needs. She had a penchant for questions that summed up lifetimes in one glint of longing:

Papa, why the music is over?

Can we just go fishing this time all our life now?

She also had a way of taking command with a sweeping claim:

I don't like bad times, Papa, I like our times.

I saw the bash men. They push you down and don't give a hug.

And sometimes she looked at exactly one thing:

The bumblebee is having a drink of water in the blue flower.

Me and Lisa are sitting on the porch watching the beetles go round and round.

I peeked and I peeked and I found a raisin in my cereal.

Sometimes she simply described her own actions, delving for understanding:

It's time for me to lie down and cry!

"Turn!" said a voice, and she turned.

When I was dancing, my feet were talking about the music.

And then there were times when her mind went off like a fire. Three instances:

[charging around the corner of the house at dusk] Dad! I came to Earth on a rocket, and you walked. Look! There are blueberries on this Earth. And look, a house! Let's go in it and see if there's a bed for me. There is! And a blankie! Look outside— raspberries! I love this Earth. It's the only one with magic. I sprinkled magic on the air and it made this Earth magic! All this stuff is new! The other Earth by Japan and Disneyland doesn't have magic. Would you like some? Here, put it in your pocket so it won't fly away. I love this one Earth. Can we live here forever?

Dad, when you sang "Clementine" my heart gave a big beat and hurt me. When my heart hears the song my heart really loves it, and so it gives a big beat because it can't talk to say it really wants to hear it again over my lifetime. I don't want to be mean for you and for us. All the people in the world have to have a chance to love and to be careful. You only have one side to be happy. Surprised is great, but scared is not. That's all. The end. You have to try!

Old Gramcracker played his cello, and he died about six months ago, but before he even died he made my hands and feet, and he is buried way up in the snowy mountains and no one can see where he is buried—up where there are twenty-two rivers and twenty-two mountains and twenty-two fires and twenty-two rocks all in a ring around where he is buried. But only the tiny birds can fly there in the morning in a summer day. His mom was an old friend of mine, too. He calls me his Gram. Dear old Gramcracker, at night he howls like an owl. I wish we could go this night to where he is buried, but we can't because there are slick mountains, and tall fires, and a river that goes a thousand miles long. Listen! "Howl!" That's Gramcracker.

My child reminds me of my childhood, and my childhood reminds me of infinite possibility, and also the beauty of limitation, the exact treasure of now:

But Dad, girls named Rosemary don't die. I'm going to be true!

You know that person bigger than everyone whose name is God? I'm hungrier than God.

The skunks blow their horns and make suddenly smoke!

More recently, our son, Guthrie, has taken over the role of the source for such expressions. At three he pointed out to us his principle for how life works:

You get what you don't want, and then the spirit of what you do want comes to you.

Or he points to a fashionably dressed woman:

Look at that lady dressed in tarantula fur!

Or he wants to help everyone:

If there were monsters in this world who never said "please," we would never know what they wanted.

And life stretches before him:

When I grow up, maybe I'll marry a deer. I could ride on his back. I wouldn't need to ride in cars or trains.

And sometimes he turns philosopher:

I wish there could be nothing, so we could have another life—no world, no space. Nothing. We could crack open nothing and be birds. Not people. We could fly.

My childhood and my children together teach me to pluck my notebook from my pocket whenever I hear language re-invented by those around me. This is my habit in class, as I listen to students try things out. For the language is old, yet strangely young. As writers, we are not called upon to be smart, but to be alert to this youth of the possible. The language is our child, our elder, our great treasure, and the writer is the one who simply takes up the lost words of daily life and gives them a book in which to dwell.

From *The Muses Among Us: Eloquent Listening and Other Pleasures of the Writer's Craft* by Kim Stafford (University of Georgia Press, 2003).

Getting Phoo Dog

Seth Loomis (fifth grade)

I lay in my bed in the dark room barely lit by a silver shot of moonlight creeping past my shade, spilling on my carpet, casting a gloomy look around my room as if nothing good would ever happen again.

"TARYN! SETH!" my dad hollered. His voice echoed through the house ricocheting off the walls. I moaned and pressed my face into the soft blue pillow. "We are going to get your mom a Christmas present!" I pretended I was asleep and didn't hear.

"Seth?!" my dad called. I stumbled out of my room—immediately engulfed by the cold air. After about six seconds I nearly froze to death and went back in my room.

"Seth, Please!" my dad snapped at me. I barely made out some mumbling outside my door. My brother stormed in nearly blowing my door off its hinges. He stomped across the ocean of junk I call my floor. He grabbed me and yanked me saying "YOU . . . NEED . . . TO . . . COME!" He dragged me out my door and down the ugly red carpet which gave me rug burn. I opened my eyes and saw my dad's brown polished shoes. I stood up.

"Can't you guys go without me? What's the point of coming?" I moaned still half asleep.

"Come On!" my dad said. As he pushed me into the car, I fell into the back seat of his new white Infiniti. Its white seats were icy cold from the long night. My dad jerked out of the garage and flew down our driveway.

"How long will it take to get there?" I grunted.

"Three or four hours!" my dad replied cheerfully. Suddenly I realized he was taking me to the dentist or maybe he was renting an educational video! I looked for an escape. But I was trapped. After five hours of boring car radio music, we pulled up to a house.

In case you skipped that I'll write it again. After five hours of boring car radio music, we pulled up to a house. You are probably getting bored so I'll return to the story.

Well, it wasn't a movie rental or the dentist so I was safe. The outside had a coating of brown paint and a small wooden porch probably added a few years after the house itself was built. The house looked ancient because of chipping paint and cracked windows. I stepped out onto the icy driveway. The cold air whipped and bit my face.

My dad walked up and hit the doorbell a few times. After a minute a tall man with a long brown beard dressed in regular blue jeans and a dark green winter jacket opened the white creaking door, revealing a small, windowless room. It had thick green fuzzy carpet, two old fashion wooden rocking chairs, and a small stone coffee table.

"Well come in!" the man said in a deep voice. We all crowded in. "Sign here, Initial here," the man said, handing my dad a paper. "Okay, Biljack," he said. Of course I was completely confuzzled. The man walked into another room. He came back holding a pillow? The "pillow" was white and yellow, almost fury looking.

I couldn't believe how long it took me to figure out what the "pillow" was. I sprang up and bounced around the room. I was overjoyed! I flew out the door. I spun across the driveway. I couldn't believe—it had been six years since we had one. As we drove home the sun painted the sky. I knew this was the best day with our new dog.

Once Upon a Twice

Denise Doyen

Once upon a twice,
In the middle of the nice,
The moon was on the rice,
And the Mice were scoutaprowl . . .

They runtunnel through the riddle—
Secret ruts hid inbetwiddle—
But, one mousling jams *the middle!*
Whilst he goofiddles, others howl:

From *Once Upon a Twice* by Denise Doyen (Random House, 2009).

Flying in the Face of Reason

Rick Reilly

One thing about life and the Big 12 basketball season: They go on. And so it was that 10 days after one of the three private planes used by the Oklahoma State team crashed, killing 10, including two players, the Cowboys had to fly again—on three private planes.

At the Stillwater airport they waded through all the dread cries of, "We'll pray for you!" and "Call the *second* you land!" They talked down the fear in their hearts and the lunch in their stomachs, deiced their nerves, tried to ignore the minicams on the tarmac and took their seats next to 10 ghosts. "Me," said an Oklahoma State student who was watching, "I'd have to be sedated."

Assistant coach Kyle Keller looked as if he was. Slit-eyed, he'd hardly slept since the night of Jan. 27, when coach Eddie Sutton had switched him out of the doomed plane for the flight home from Colorado and sat Keller's cousin, freshman point guard Nate Fleming, in his place. Sutton wanted Keller on the faster jet instead of the turboprop so Keller could get back to Stillwater a half hour earlier and start grading film. Now Fleming was gone. "I don't go 10 seconds without thinking about it," said Keller, who had to pull over on the interstate between funerals last week and sob for 20 minutes. "Someday, I'm hoping God explains this all to me."

The guy sitting behind him now, broadcaster Tom Dirato, knew the feeling. Sutton had switched Dirato from the turboprop to the jet, so he and his aching back wouldn't have to sit so long, and put junior guard Danny Lawson in Dirato's place. Now Lawson is in a grave in Detroit. "I go from grief to relief," said Dirato, who will undergo counseling starting this week. "I'm 56. Danny was 21. He had his whole life in front of him."

As the cabin door closed, 7-foot freshman center Jack Marlow was thinking the same thing. He'd always hated to fly, but when the crash killed his road roomie, Lawson, his fear doubled. Sutton had asked the players if they wanted to take the

55-minute flight or the eight-hour bus ride to Lincoln for their game against Nebraska, and Big Jack had yelped, "Bus sounds great, Coach!" But he was the only one. So as the Lear engine revved, he stuck his Choctaw mandala in the window, kissed it once, bowed his huge head and started praying.

Two planes back, 280-pound center Jason Keep clamped assistant coach Sean Sutton's hand so tight it went numb. Not that Sean, Eddie's son, wanted Keep to let go. Every time he closes his eyes, he imagines the inside of that turboprop, beelining nose-first for a Colorado pasture. "I can't stop seeing them," said Sutton, whose best friend, director of basketball operations Pat Noyes, died in the wreckage. "Did they know they were going to die? Were they screaming? Panicking? I have nightmares about it."

Last to buckle in was Eddie Sutton, the 64-year-old coaching legend who had to call the 10 wives and mothers and fathers and girlfriends that night and tell them their men weren't coming home. Sutton said he carries no guilt over having changed the seating arrangement. "We've switched 100 times, every trip, for 100 reasons," he said. But those calls, those funerals, those what-ifs have added 10 years to his face. His friends worry about him. Bill Clinton called to check on him. "Eddie's in denial," said Patsy, his wife. "He's had to be so strong for everyone else, he hasn't been able to grieve."

Well, my God, where would you start? With Will Hancock, the sports information assistant who loved Beethoven, his soccer-coach wife and his two-month-old baby? Or student manager Jared Weiberg, who was making his last scheduled road trip of the season? Or radio engineer Kendall Durfey, who with his wife had just adopted a little girl whose parents had died? Or trainer Brian Luinstra, who had two kids under three? Or the two pilots, Denver Mills and Bjorn Fahlstrom? Who has that many tears?

Now the jet engines shudder, and now the planes lurch, and now it's wheels up. And now, for the first time in his life, star point guard Maurice Baker's hands drip wet on a flight. And now Dirato remembers that his dead colleague, play-by-play man Bill Teegins, had a commercial ticket home from Denver before a spot opened up on the turboprop. Talk about luck: Turns out the commercial flight was canceled because of the bad weather.

This time, of course, nothing happened, not a bump. All three planes made it safely to Lincoln, where the Cowboys lost to Nebraska 78-75 in overtime.

The newspaper said they had trouble rebounding.

The Poetry of J. Patrick Lewis

J. Patrick Lewis believes that no child should be denied the magic of wordplay: "If we are trying to encourage them to be writers/poets, why shouldn't we show them the amazing legerdemain, the extremes to which language can and should be taken? We don't encourage them to be novelists and then deny them the classics. So why should we shield them from all the tricks available to them?"

A Balding Pig

A rare and hairless Hampshire Pig
Came in my shop today.
I made the pig a piggy-wig
But he forgot toupee.

Dead Weight

Everyone knew that
He was rich and fat,
But no one ever learned
How much he urned.

Tom Tigercat

Tom Tigercat is noted
for his manners and his wit.
He wouldn't think of lion,
No, he doesn't cheetah bit.

Tom never has pretended
to be something that he's not.
I guess that's why we like him
and why he likes ocelot.

There Was an Old Woman

There was an old woman
Who lived in a sneaker.
She had so many Keds
Her life was getting bleaker.
She tied their shoelaces
Together for fun
And now those poor Keds
Have nowhere to run.

Animal Epitaphs

For a Sheep

No one will ever forget ewe

For a Boll Weevil

Gone but not for cotton

For a Skunk

He won't be mist

For a Pigeon

She was pooped

For a Moth

In case I come back,
Leave the porch light on

For a Mouse

Miss the traps
Miss the cheese
Miss the cheddars
Miss the bries
Miss the Colbys
Miss the Swisses
Miss the Muensters
Miss the Mrs.

Epitaph for a Pitcher

No runs,
No hits,
No heirs

Epitaph for Pinocchio

Here lies

American Autumn

O

H,

O

A

K

T

R

E

E,

Y

O

U

L

E

F

T

SUCH

A HEAP!

THE FRONT-

YARD   LEAVES

ARE GETTING DEEP

AND I HAVE PREMISES

TO KEEP AND PILES TO

GO THAT I MUST SWEEP AND

PILES TO GO THAT I MUST SWEEP

Alphabet Game

Mickey played golf and T'd the ball.
Matty played pool and Q'd the ball.
Andy played catch and I'd the ball.
Timmy played a baby and P'd is all.

The Hangman Shouts
A One-Word Poem

NECKST!

How To Tell a Camel

The Dromedary has one hump,
The Bactrian has two.
It's easy to forget this rule,
So here is what to do.
Roll the first initial over
On its flat behind:

The ꞵ actrian is different from
The ꓷ romedary kind.

Where Can You Find a New Nose?

Ralph Fletcher

If you need a new eye
Try the eye of a needle.

If you need a new neck
Try the neck of a bottle.

There are extra-sharp teeth
On the blade of a saw.

    But where can you find a new nose, a new nose?
    Who knows where to find a new nose?

You will find a new head
At the top of your bed . . .

. . . Or can get a new foot
With twelve inches instead.

There's a nice soft shoulder
At the edge of the road.

    But where you can you find a new nose, a new nose?
    Who knows where to find a new nose?

Would you like a new lip?
Check the edge of a cup.

Need a fresh face?
Check the front of a clock.

You might get a new tongue
Tucked inside your shoe.

> *But where can you find a new nose, a new nose?*
> *Who knows where to find a new nose?*

If you'd like a new mouth
Try the mouth of a cave.

You'll find some new curls
In the swirl of a wave.

There are plenty of ears
In a tall field of corn.

> *But where can you find a new nose, a new nose?*
> *Who knows where to find a new nose?*

Snicking Up the Rug

Ralph Fletcher

With such a big family, Mom and Dad created lots of rituals to keep the family running smoothly. But some of our rituals were a little odd, like when Mom motioned us into the living room and told us to "snick up" the rug.

"Aw, Mom," Jimmy moaned. "I want to go outside."

"C'mon," she said. "It won't take five minutes."

At that word—*snick*—each of us got down on all fours and started picking up tiny bits of dirt, dust, and lint from the rug. I grabbed a piece of dirt, tucked it neatly into my palm, and scooted forward to pick up some more. Everyone helped; even the baby pitched in. With so many kids, plus Mom, it didn't take long before the rug looked nice and clean again.

The same ritual took place every night, and I never gave it a second thought. It's not as if we were poor. We had a TV and a car. We had a vacuum cleaner, too, but for some reason we never used it at the end of the day. Instead, we snicked. And I figured that the same thing must be happening in every other house in town—mothers and kids getting down on their knees to snick up the rug before Dad got home from work.

From *Marshfield Dreams: When I Was a Kid* by Ralph Fletcher (Henry Holt, 2005).

Beach Baby

Ralph Fletcher

She's one year old. One tooth. A total pudge.
She tries to get out of the water but her
soaked diaper must weigh
ten thousand pounds
so all she can do is
sit.

Later she sees me eating Cheese Puffs
and toddles over, towering above me,
a baby so giant she blocks out the sun,
sticks out her hand and yells: "Mine's!"

Her mother hurries over, apologizes,
and drags her back to their blanket.
The baby starts eating sand, grinning,
grinding the grains with that one tooth.

Chocolate

Max Gilmore (sixth grade)

Did you ever crave more chocolate than you can handle? Well, I did once at my twin little brothers' 6th birthday party, and it wasn't pretty. The culprit? A compelling chocolate fountain that my mom's friend had loaned us. The victim? Me.

After we melted the chunks of chocolate slowly in the fountain base and had got the "waterfall" of melted chocolate running like the instructions showed us, my mom put me in charge because I asked for the job. She was busy keeping the little kids from getting too wild in the house. Finally, I was able to play with the chocolate as much as I wanted. It was entertaining to see what I could make out of what seemed to be an infinite amount of CHOCOLATE! Also it was fun to share the chocolate with little kids and see how excited they were by it. Maybe their enthusiasm rubbed off on me . . . soon I was in the grips of a full-on chocolate frenzy.

Everything was great at first. So much chocolate. I was in hog heaven. I couldn't stop trying out new combinations of weirder and weirder stuff to dip in. Carrots, bread, apples, cheese, even finger when I ran out of those! The best combination was the fresh strawberries dipped in the fountain. Mmmmm, I can taste it now. The scariest combination was when my friend Joe invented the "Spoonful Of Hyper" dessert made with pure sugar dipped into the chocolate fountain. Of course, this is coming from a kid who puts about eight spoonfuls of sugar in his tea or coffee.

Then, gradually, I began to feel sick and shake all over. My stomach felt like an over-inflated balloon that was about to pop! I felt miserable. Was there a lesson to be learned? Were my eyes bigger than my stomach? (1st moral). Yes, but I'd do it again in a heartbeat. Soon the sick feeling passed, but the joyful memories remained. And I guess I am lucky to have a fast metabolism. Isn't chocolate supposed to be good for you these days, anyway? My 2nd moral: "eat as much chocolate as possible at every opportunity."

Owl Pellets

Ralph Fletcher

A month ago
in biology lab
you sat close to me
knee touching mine
your sweet smell
almost drowning out
the formaldehyde stink
which crinkled up
your nose
while I dissected
our fetal pig.

Now I take apart
this owl pellet
small bag that holds
skin and hair and bones
little skeletons
what the owl ate
but couldn't digest
and coughed back up.

You sit with Jon Fox
ignore me completely
laugh at his dumb jokes
let your head fall onto
his bony shoulder

while I attempt
to piece together
with trembling hands
the tiny bones
of a baby snake.

Certain things
are just about
impossible
to swallow.

Sledding Disaster

Version 1

On Saturday I went sledding at Wagon Hill. My little brother Austin was on my back. First we were going at a regular speed. Then we were going faster and faster. My brother was clinging to my neck. I was clutching the sled. Then I realized we were going too fast. I tried to use the brake but it wouldn't work. I couldn't think of anything to do. We swerved to the left and the right. I yelled to Austin to hang on tight. But we wiped out halfway down the hill.

Version 2

Last Saturday I went sledding at Wagon Hill with my little brother Austin on my back. At first we were going at regular speed, but soon we started moving faster and faster. My brother was clinging to my neck while I clutched the sled. Both of us held on for dear life, trying to go straight, but I realized we were going too fast. I tried the brake. Nothing! What's this? It didn't work! No! Whoa, what now? We swerved to the left. Oh, Mama. Then to the right. Oh, Doctor! Hang on, Austin! Crash! Bang! Wipeout!

Bibliography

Children's Books

Agee, Jon. 1991. *Go Hang a Salami! I'm a Lasagna Hog! And Other Palindromes.* New York: Farrar, Straus and Giroux.

——. 2002. *Palindromania!* New York: Farrar, Straus and Giroux.

——. 2006. *Smart Feller Fart Smeller: And Other Spoonerisms.* New York: Hyperion.

Ahlberg, Janet and Allan. 1986. *Each Peach Pear Plum.* New York: Penguin.

Aliki. 1987. *The Two of Them.* New York: HarperCollins.

Amato, Mary. 2008. *Please Write in This Book.* New York: Holiday House.

Anthony, Piers. 1987. *A Spell for Chameleon: The First Xanth Novel.* New York: Del Ray.

Atwell, Debby. 2001. *Barn.* New York: Sandpiper.

Babbitt, Natalie. 2007. *Tuck Everlasting.* New York: Square Fish.

Barretta, Gene. 2007. *Dear Deer: A Book of Homophones.* New York: Henry Holt.

Baum, L. Frank. 2000. *The Wizard of Oz.* New York: Random House.

Bemelmans, Ludwig. 1977. *Madeline.* New York: Picture Puffins.

Bloch, Serge. 2008. *Butterflies in My Stomach and Other School Hazards.* New York: Sterling.

Borden, Louise. 2003. *The Little Ships: The Heroic Rescue at Dunkirk in World War II.* New York: Aladdin.

———. 2005. *The Journey That Saved Curious George: The True War-Time Escape of Margret and H. A. Rey*. Boston: Houghton Mifflin.

Byng, Georgia. 2006. *Molly Moon's Hypnotic Time Travel Adventure*. New York: HarperCollins.

Carroll, Lewis. 2000. "Jabberwocky." In *Alice's Adventures in Wonderland and Through the Looking Glass*. New York: Signet Classics.

Cleary, Brian P. 2005. *How Much Can a Bare Bear Bear: What Are Homonyms and Homophones?* Brookfield, CT: Millbrook.

Clements, Andrew. 1998. *Frindle*. New York: Aladdin.

Cole, Joanna. 1992. *The Magic School Bus* series. New York: Scholastic.

Crutcher, Chris. 2001. *Whale Talk*. New York: HarperCollins.

———. 2003. *The Crazy Horse Electric Game*. New York: Harper.

———. 2006. *The Sledding Hill*. New York: Harper Teen.

Cummings, Priscilla. 2006. *Red Kayak*. New York: Puffin.

Curtis, Christopher Paul. 2000. *The Watsons Go to Birmingham—1963*. New York: Laurel-Leaf.

Dahl, Roald. 2007a. *The BFG*. New York: Puffin.

———. 2007b. *Charlie and the Chocolate Factory*. New York: Puffin.

dePaola, Tomie. 1975. *Strega Nona*. New York: Aladdin.

Doyen, Denise. 2009. *Once Upon a Twice*. New York: Random House.

Ernst, Lisa Campbell. *Goldilocks Returns*. New York: Simon and Schuster.

Fletcher, Ralph. 1994. "Owl Pellets." In *I Am Wings: Poems About Love*. New York: Atheneum.

———. 1996. *Fig Pudding*. New York: Clarion.

———. 1997a. *Ordinary Things: Poems from a Walk in Spring*. New York: Atheneum.

———. 1997b. *Twilight Comes Twice*. New York: Clarion.

———. 1998. *Flying Solo*. New York: Clarion.

———. 2003. *Hello, Harvest Moon*. New York: Clarion.

———. 2005a. *Marshfield Dreams: When I Was a Kid*. New York: Henry Holt.

———. 2005b. "Bad Weather." In *A Writing Kind of Day*. Honesdale, PA: Boyds Mills Press.

———. 2006. *The Sandman*. New York: Henry Holt.

Florian, Douglas. 1999. "Maskquito" and "Inventions I'd Like to See." In *Laugheteria*. San Diego: Harcourt.

Franco, Betsy. 2009. "Symmetricats." In *A Curious Collection of Cats*. Berkeley, CA: Tricycle Press.

Gutman, Dan. 2008a. *Mrs. Dole Is Out of Control!* My Weird School Daze 1. New York: HarperCollins.

———. 2008b. *Nightmare at the Book Fair*. New York: Simon and Schuster.

———. 2009. *Officer Spence Makes No Sense!* My Weird School Daze 5. New York: HarperCollins.

Henkes, Kevin. 2004. *Kitten's First Full Moon*. New York: Greenwillow.

Hoban, Russell. 1970. *A Bargain for Frances*. New York: Harper and Row.

Johnston, Tony. 1996. *The Cowboy and the Black-Eyed Pea*. New York: Putnam.

Juster, Norton. 1961. *The Phantom Tollbooth*. New York: Random House.

Kimmel, Eric A. 1990. *Four Dollars and Fifty Cents*. New York: Holiday House.

Kinnell, Galway. 2008. "Burning the Brush Pile." In *Strong Is Your Hold: Poems*. New York: Mariner Books.

Krosoczka, Jarrett J. 2009a. *Lunch Lady and the League of Librarians*. New York: Knopf.

———. 2009b. *Lunch Lady and the Cyborg Substitute*. New York: Knopf.

Laden, Nina. 1995. *Private I. Guana: The Case of the Missing Chameleon*. San Francisco: Chronicle Books.

———. 2000. *Roberto the Insect Architect*. San Francisco: Chronicle Books.

Lederer, Richard. 1996. *Pun and Games: Jokes, Riddles, Daffynitions, Tairy Fales, Rhymes, and More Word Play for Kids*. Chicago: Chicago Review.

Lewis, J. Patrick. 1990. *A Hippopotamusn't*. New York: Dial.

———. 2009. *Countdown to Summer: A Poem for Every Day of the School Year*. New York: Little, Brown.

Lowry, Lois. 2008. *The Willoughbys*. New York: Houghton Mifflin.

Lubar, David. 2006. *Punished!* Plain City, OH: Darby Creek.

Martin, Bill Jr., and John Archambault. 1997. *Knots on a Counting Rope*. New York: Henry Holt.

———. 2009. *Chicka Chicka Boom Boom*. New York: Beach Lane Books.

McDonald, Megan. 2007. *Stink and the Incredible Super-Galactic Jawbreaker*. Somerville, MA: Candlewick.

McMullan, Kate. 2002. *I Stink!* New York: HarperCollins.

———. 2006. *I'm Dirty!* New York: HarperCollins.

Merriam, Eve. 1964. "Onomatopoeia." In *It Doesn't Always Have to Rhyme*. New York: Atheneum.

Miranda, Anne. 1996. *Pignic: An Alphabet Book in Rhyme*. Honesdale, PA: Boyds Mills Press.

O'Malley, Kevin. 2007. *Gimme Cracked Corn and I Will Share*. New York: Walker.

Palatini, Margie. 1995. *Piggie Pie!* New York: Sandpiper.

Paterson, Katherine. 1987. *The Great Gilly Hopkins.* New York: HarperCollins.

Piven, Hanoch. 2007. *My Dog Is as Smelly as Dirty Socks: And Other Funny Family Portraits.* New York: Schwartz and Wade.

Poe, Edgar Allan. 1975. "Annabel Lee." In *Complete Tales and Poems of Edgar Allan Poe.* New York: Vintage Books.

Ringgold, Faith. 1996. *Tar Beach.* Dragonfly Books.

Rowling, J. K. 1998–2007. The Harry Potter series. New York: Scholastic.

Rylant, Cynthia. 1985. *The Relatives Came.* New York: Atheneum.

Scieszka, Jon. 2004. *Summer Reading Is Killing Me!* New York: Puffin.

Sendak, Maurice. 1988. *Where the Wild Things Are.* New York: HarperCollins.

Seuss, Dr. 1961. *The Sneetches and Other Stories.* New York: Random House.

———. 1971. *The Lorax.* New York: Random House.

———. 1984. *The Butter Battle Book.* New York: Random House.

———. 2004. *Horton Hatches an Egg.* New York: Random House.

Shannon, David. 1998. *No, David!* New York: The Blue Sky Press.

Shulman, Mark. 2006. *Mom and Dad Are Palindromes.* San Francisco: Chronicle Books.

Silverstein, Shel. 2005. *Runny Babbit: A Billy Sook.* New York: HarperCollins.

Snicket, Lemony. 1999–2006. A Series of Unfortunate Events, Books 1–13. New York: HarperCollins.

Spinelli, Jerry. 1990. *Maniac Magee.* New York: Little, Brown.

Steig, William. 1971. *Amos & Boris*. New York: Farrar, Straus and Giroux.

———. 1986. *Gorky Rises*. New York: Farrar, Straus and Giroux.

———. 1988. *Brave Irene*. New York: Farrar, Straus and Giroux.

———. 1990. *Shrek!* New York: Michael Di Capua Books.

Stevens, Janet, and Susan Stevens Crummel. 2001. *And the Dish Ran Away with the Spoon*. San Diego: Harcourt.

———. 2005. *The Great Fuzz Frenzy*. San Diego: Harcourt.

Tabor, Nancy Maria Grande. 2000. *Ve Lo Que Dices/See What You Say*. Watertown, MA: Charlesbridge.

Tennyson, Alfred, Lord. 2008. "Come Down, O Maid." In *Selected Poems*. New York: Penguin.

Terban, Marvin. 1993. *It Figures! Fun Figures of Speech*. New York: Sandpiper.

Trine, Greg. 2007. *The Fake Cape Caper*. Melvin Beederman, Superhero. New York: Henry Holt.

———. 2008. *Attack of the Valley Girls*. Melvin Beederman, Superhero. New York: Henry Holt.

Twain, Mark. 1994. *The Adventures of Tom Sawyer*. New York: Penguin.

Ward, Lynd. 1952. *The Biggest Bear*. Boston: Houghton Mifflin.

Wood, Audrey. 1982. *Quick as a Cricket*. Swindon, England: Child's Play International.

Yolen, Jane. 1987. *Owl Moon*. New York: Philomel.

———. 1996. *Encounter*. New York: Voyager.

Other Suggested Children's Books

Additional Wordplay Books by Jon Agee

Elvis Lives! And Other Anagrams. 2000. New York: Farrar, Straus and Giroux.

Orangutan Tongs: Poems to Tangle Your Tongue. 2009. New York: Hyperion.

Sit on a Potato Pan, Otis! More Palindromes. 1999. New York: Farrar, Straus and Giroux.

So Many Dynamos! And Other Palindromes. 1994. New York: Farrar, Straus and Giroux.

Who Ordered the Jumbo Shrimp? And Other Oxymorons. 1998. New York: HarperCollins.

Picture Books That Model Language Play or a Love of Words

Banks, Kate. 2006. *Max's Words*. New York: Farrar, Straus and Giroux.

Cleary, Brian P. 2006. *Rhyme and Punishment: Adventures in Wordplay*. Minneapolis, MN: Millbrook Press.

Deedy, Carmen Agra. 1994. *Agatha's Featherbed: Not Just Another Wild Goose Story*. Atlanta: Peachtree Publishers.

Keller, Laurie. 2000. *Open Wide: Tooth School Inside*. New York: Henry Holt.

Schotter, Roni. 2006. *The Boy Who Loved Words*. New York: Schwartz and Wade.

Picture Books for Younger Readers (4–7) That Play with Words

Bryan, Sean. 2005. *A Boy and His Bunny*. New York: Arcade Publishing.

Cousins, Lucy. 2008. *Hooray for Fish!* Cambridge, MA: Candlewick Press.

Ehlert, Lois. 2006. *In My World*. New York: Voyager.

Gravett, Emily. 2007. *Orange Pear Apple Bear*. New York: Simon and Schuster. (An entire story told using only five words.)

Seeger, Laura Vaccaro. 2006. *Walter Was Worried*. New Milford, CT: Roaring Brook Press.

———. 2008. *One Boy*. New Milford, CT: Roaring Brook Press.

Yolen, Jane. 2000. *Off We Go!* Boston: Little, Brown.

Books About Expressions and Sayings

Brennan-Nelson, Denise. 2004. *My Teacher Likes to Say*. Chelsea, MI: Sleeping Bear Press.

Brisson, Pat. 2004. *Beach Is to Fun: A Book of Relationships*. New York: Henry Holt.

Gwynne, Fred. 1988. *The King Who Rained*. New York: Aladdin.

———. 2005. *A Chocolate Moose for Dinner*. New York: Aladdin.

Leedy, Loreen. 2009. *Crazy Like a Fox: A Simile Story*. New York: Holiday House.

Leedy, Loreen, and Pat Street. 2003. *There's a Frog in My Throat: 440 Animal Sayings a Little Bird Told Me*. New York: Holiday House.

Scanlon, Elizabeth Garton. 2004. *A Sock Is a Pocket for Your Toes: A Pocket Book*. New York: HarperCollins.

Terban, Marvin. 2006. *Scholastic Dictionary of Idioms*. New York: Scholastic Reference.

———. 2007. *In a Pickle: And Other Funny Idioms*. New York: Sandpiper.

Ziefert, Harriet. 2005. *Misery Is a Smell in Your Backpack*. Maplewood, NJ: Blue Apple Books.

Adult Books and Articles

Benbow, Julian. 2008. "One to Remember." *The Boston Globe*, January 5.

Britton, James. 1970. *Language and Learning*. London: Penguin.

Bruner, Jerome. 1984. "Language, Mind, and Reading." In *Awakening to Literacy*, ed. Antoinette Oberg, Hillel Goelman, and Frank Smith. Portsmouth, NH: Heinemann.

———. 1992. *Acts of Meaning*. Cambridge, MA: Harvard University Press.

Bryson, Bill. 1990. *The Mother Tongue*. New York: HarperCollins.

Buckner, Aimee. 2005. *Notebook Know-How*. Portland, ME: Stenhouse.

Chatwin, Bruce. 1988. *The Songlines*. New York: Penguin.

Chiaro, Delia. 1992. *The Language of Jokes: Analysing Verbal Play*. New York: Routledge.

Cook, Guy. 2000. *Language Play, Language Learning*. Oxford, England: Oxford University Press.

Crystal, David. 1998. *Language Play*. Chicago: University of Chicago Press.

———. 2006. *Words, Words, Words*. Oxford, England: Oxford University Press.

Csikszentmihalyi, Mihaly. 1994. *The Evolving Self*. New York: Harper.

Davis, Ivor. 1999. "Q & A: Matt Groening." E! Online. http://www.eonline.com/Celebs/Qa/Groening/.

Feigelson, Dan. 2008. *Practical Punctuation: Lessons on Rule Making and Rule Breaking in Elementary Writing*. Portsmouth, NH: Heinemann.

Fletcher, Ralph. 1993. *What a Writer Needs*. Portsmouth, NH: Heinemann.

———. 1996. *Breathing In, Breathing Out: Keeping a Writer's Notebook*. Portsmouth, NH: Heinemann.

Fletcher, Ralph, and JoAnn Portalupi. 2001. *Writing Workshop: The Essential Guide*. Portsmouth, NH: Heinemann.

———. 2007. *Craft Lessons: Teaching Writing K–8*. 2nd ed. Portland, ME: Stenhouse.

Gladwell, Malcolm. 2008. "Most Likely to Succeed." *The New Yorker*, December 5.

Glass, Julia. 2003. *Three Junes*. New York: Anchor Books.

Greene, Graham. 1992. *A Burnt-Out Case*. New York: Penguin Classics.

Hall, Rich. 1985. *More Sniglets: (Snig'lit), Any Word That Doesn't Appear in the Dictionary, But Should*. New York: Collier.

Hemingway, Ernest. 1981. *The Old Man and the Sea*. New York: Simon and Schuster.

Hornby, Nick. 1995. *High Fidelity*. New York: Penguin.

Kaysen, Susanna. 1995. *Girl, Interrupted*. New York: Vintage.

McCarthy, Cormac. 1995. *The Crossing*. New York: Vintage.

Murray, Donald M. 1989. *Expecting the Unexpected: Teaching Myself—and Others—To Read and Write*. Portsmouth, NH: Boynton Cook.

Newkirk, Thomas. 2009. *Holding On to Good Ideas in a Time of Bad Ones*. Portsmouth, NH: Heinemann.

Oberg, Antoinette, Hillel Goelman, and Frank Smith. 1984. *Awakening to Literacy*. Portsmouth, NH: Heinemann.

Reilly, Rick. 2001. "Flying in the Face of Reason." *Sports Illustrated*, February 19.

Robbins, Tom. 1990. *Even Cowgirls Get the Blues*. New York: Bantam.

Shaughnessy, Dan. 2004. *The Curse of the Bambino*. New York: Penguin.

———. 2007. "No Dramatic Event, Just a Mini-Series." *The Boston Globe*, August 29.

———. "Back on Top." 2008. *The Boston Globe*, June 18.

———. 2009. "Blair Gave Musketeers Bum's Rush." *The Boston Globe*, March 27.

Stafford, Kim. 2003. *The Muses Among Us: Eloquent Listening and Other Pleasures of the Writer's Craft*. Athens: University of Georgia Press.

Szymusiak, Karen, Franki Sibberson, and Lisa Koch. 2008. *Beyond Leveled Books*. 2nd ed. Portland, ME: Stenhouse.

Vygotsky, L. S. 1978. *Mind in Society: The Development of Higher Psychological Processes*. Cambridge, MA: Harvard University Press.

Wallace, Robert. 1991. *Writing Poems*. 3rd ed. New York: HarperCollins.

Wallraff, Barbara. 2006. *Word Fugitives: In Pursuit of Wanted Words*. New York: Collins.